D1002770

WHAT KEEPS US SOBER

Written by Recovering Alcoholics and Drug Addicts
for Recovering Alcoholics and Drug Addicts

whatkeepsussober.com

ROLAND LEVY LMHC

3 1969 02385 1412

ISBN: 978-1-4834-3534-3 (sc)
ISBN: 978-1-4834-3533-6 (e)

Library of Congress Control Number: 2015911683

Lulu Publishing Services rev. date: 10/26/2015

DEDICATION

This book is dedicated to suffering. The suffering that led us to our addiction, the suffering throughout our addiction, and the ability to deal with life on life's terms.

TABLE OF CONTENTS

INTRODUCTION

To the alcoholic or drug addict, the need to get clean and sober is widely recognized. This only represents part of the battle. The need to remain clean and sober should be the ultimate goal. Would getting clean and/or sober be viewed as a worthy undertaking if relapse were already a consideration at the outset? When I was in treatment I was told that relapse was part of the process. This may have been to reduce feelings of incompetence, failure, frustration and hopelessness. The alcoholic or drug addict may conclude that to get clean and/or sober is no more than an exercise in futility, since relapse represents an integral part of sobriety. This may discourage any attempt at recovery for some, while, for others, it may encourage them to give up when they are most vulnerable since relapse is part of the process and must be accepted as such. This clearly represents a misinterpretation of the aforementioned concept in order to satisfy the needs of the addictive mind. Are faulty reasoning and illogical, irrational thinking not an integral part of the addictive process?

While this book does not represent a lifetime guarantee for sobriety, if some of its concepts are closely adhered to it will, at least, reduce the number of relapse episodes while giving hope to the reader that relapse is not inevitable, and is, in fact, avoidable. While it may be assumed that a book presumed to keep drug addicts and alcoholics clean and sober is intended only for those who have already achieved intermediate to long-term sobriety, the information provided has already proved to be effective by the co-authors of this book and can be used by <u>anyone</u> seeking guidance and help in developing a clean and sober lifestyle.

The book originated from a sobriety group in which each member was asked: "What keeps you sober?" While the group has been ongoing since 2001, the information was gathered from 2005 to 2008. The group meets weekly and is free of charge to members of the community. Over a three-year period the length of time of membership varied from just one session to the full three-year period. Sobriety in the group varied from just one day to 24 years, with some of the original members still attending the group. In order to maintain equal status with other group members, I chose to participate in the group as a member and not a facilitator. All members were encouraged to bring in material that may benefit the group.

While the group members acted as co-authors in supplying the individual headings of this book, I was responsible for the text. I hope that the text represents an accurate representation of the context in which the headings were provided by each member. It was always my intention to remain faithful to the original meaning. At times, however, my interpretation had to be invoked. I apologize for those times. While individual credit is not given to any members in order to protect their anonymity, their contribution remains, however, no less appreciated.

It was once said that to the recovering alcoholic or drug addict, there are only two things in life: actively drinking or using and practicing relapse prevention. I hope that this book will provide a useful tool to its readers and that the treacherous road of sobriety will be more attainable thanks to the experiences of this book's co-authors.

In conclusion, this book demonstrates some of the many different means of keeping sober. In addition to those methods described in this book, there are a great deal more that the reader may already be using or will discover in the future. It is recommended for the reader to incorporate those and any others he or she might find useful into their recovery. Prior to our addiction, we were all different individuals with some commonalities. Since recovery is a journey of personal discovery, it stands to reason that each alcoholic or addict's recovery plan is customized to their individual personal needs and likes. May your recovery plan be rewarding and satisfying to curb any appetite, however fleeting, for the addictive forces within.

ROLAND LEVY, LMHC

SEEING THE EFFECTS OF OUR ADDICTION ON OUR LOVED ONES –

This includes how our addictions have caused the distancing of our friends and families, resulting in broken families, separation, and divorce. Alienation of family and friends can often be the result of addiction. Addiction also increases the likelihood of conflict and causes an imbalance in relationships.

EXERCISE –

Exercise can play a crucial role in recovery. Through exercise, we derive a sense of well-being. Exercise represents the most effective method for stress management. Since stress is the leading factor in relapse for both substance abuse and mental illness, it becomes essential that exercise becomes part of our daily routines. You don't have time for exercise? You sure had time for drinking and/or using! Exercise also allows us to begin physical recovery. Through exercise, we increase our heart rates and our lung capacities and improve circulation. If the exercise happens to be aerobic, we can even experience the sensation of becoming high. Not a euphoric high, but a general feeling of elation that can remain throughout the day through the release of endorphins.

FAMILY –

Family can be part of the solution. Family can also be part of the problem. A loving, caring, supporting family can represent the environment in which recovery can take place. Also, in the early stages of recovery, the alcoholic or drug addict is very vulnerable. When family members refrain from drinking/using in the presence of the alcoholic or drug addict, this can reduce cravings and facilitate sobriety.

On the other hand, family members who create conflict as opposed to resolving it increase the level of stress for the alcoholic or drug addict. Getting sober alone and giving up familiar behavior and replacing it with new behavior can be stressful enough.

FEAR OF COMING DOWN IN JAIL –

For the alcoholic or drug addict, jail is often a familiar place. As alcohol and drugs are abused in increasing amounts, the need for a medically supervised detoxification can become necessary. Incarceration can pose a serious risk to someone in need of detoxification. Also, medication that has been prescribed by a physician is often not given in jail. This can cause the alcoholic or drug addict to become psychiatrically unstable and more vulnerable to relapse.

FEAR OF LOSING ALL THAT HAS BEEN GAINED IN SOBRIETY –

This is a very realistic fear. When the alcoholic or drug addict experiences a lapse or minor relapse, he or she cannot predict in advance the severity of the relapse. If we are unable to return to sobriety, the consequences can be monumental. Also, the fear of losing all that has been gained in sobriety does not fully represent the magnitude of addiction. In fact, the reality of losing *more* than we have gained in sobriety must also be contemplated.

RECOVERY LITERATURE –

Without necessarily becoming experts in the field of addiction, it is important to learn as much as we can about the effects our addictions have on us. This can create an awareness without which it becomes difficult to understand what is going on and why. Recovery literature can be found in recovery meetings, self-help sections of bookstores, or on the Internet.

It is important to recognize that not all information will be useful. I once found useful information on the very last page of a book I read! Become discriminatory. We must also be very selective as to what we use. Remember—recovery literature is not written with one particular individual in mind. It is intended to appeal to a very broad readership.

KEEPING BUSY –

When we have too much idle time, our minds tend to shift to topics related to our addiction. This increases the likelihood of relapse. In contrast, when we first begin to experience cravings, keeping busy reduces the impact the cravings have on us and lessens the risk of relapse. Some of the activities we can use include calling a friend in recovery, reading recovery literature, attending a meeting, or engaging in some form of physical activity. Relaxation and meditation can also play a role in relapse prevention.

FRIENDS –

Friends can provide the support and encouragement we need in order to remain on the path of sobriety. Also, following lapses or relapses, friends can provide us with the impetus to get back on track. It is important, however, to distinguish between those friends who respect our decision to be clean and sober and those "friends" who would just as soon sabotage our recovery for selfish motives, in order to have someone to drink or get high with. True friends will not drink or use drugs in the presence of the recovering person. Their friendship will be based on common interests and activities unrelated to drugs and alcohol.

MARRIAGE –

Marriage can provide motivation for recovery. While long-term recovery cannot be based on external factors, marriage can represent an introduction to treatment. For the treatment to be successful, there must eventually be a conversion from external to internal motivation. Marriage will usually have a positive impact on sobriety, when one partner is supportive of the other's attempt at sobriety. If both partners in the marriage are either alcoholic or addicted to drugs, sobriety by either partner can be substantially compromised.

GARDENING –

Gardening is a relaxing activity that reduces stress and anxiety, both triggers to relapse. Gardening also takes place in nature, and the ability to make something grow and to care for something other than oneself has a sobering effect. The act of weeding, which many gardeners find unfulfilling, can have a peaceful, soothing effect on the recovering person. It is not unusual for recovering alcoholics and drug addicts to create and maintain some of the best gardens in their neighborhoods.

HELPING OTHERS –

In order to maintain an addiction, a certain amount of selfishness is required. In order to achieve sobriety, help is often required from others. Sobriety can be viewed as a gift. This gift is to be passed on and shared with others. The simple act of giving allows us to feel fulfilled and replenishes the self-esteem that had been so severely depleted by our addictions.

DESIRE FOR LOST EXCELLENCE –

Addiction to drugs or alcohol can be viewed as the great equalizer. The more one has, the more one has to lose. Intelligence, wealth, creative ability, equilibrium, reflexes, eloquence, coordination, control, judgment, inhibition, sleep, sexual performance, values, and family are all negatively impacted by our addictions. Sobriety allows us to regain some of the losses and possibly achieve excellence once again.

AVOIDING WITHDRAWAL SYMPTOMS –

Many alcoholics and drug addicts maintain addiction in order to avoid withdrawal. Those who are successful in their sobriety have a strong recollection of the negative effect withdrawal had on them. Some are even able to access this recollection when they are experiencing cravings. This may serve as a deterrent and, when successful, allow sobriety to remain intact.

ENGAGING IN PLEASURABLE ACTIVITIES –

In the initial stages of sobriety, we are faced with a great deal of time that was previously occupied by our addictions. Engaging in pleasurable activities represents a viable alternative to our addictions. Many alcoholics and drug addicts suffer from depression. Anhedonia, or the inability to engage in pleasurable activities, can decrease the quality of life for many alcoholics and drug addicts. When they recover from their addictions, engaging in pleasurable activities can counteract depressive tendencies resulting from their addictions.

SURVIVAL –

Whether we are willing to face our mortality or not, we are all going to die. We do, however, have a choice if we want to die sooner—or later. Some alcoholics and drug addicts feel that death represents the end of their suffering, without even stopping to consider that sobriety too can represent that end. It has been said that addiction represents death on the installment plan. We know that long-term addiction will result in impairment of vital organs. What we don't know is when this will occur and which organs will be impacted. While some damage may be irreversible, our bodies have the remarkable ability to recover from years of abuse and neglect. Sobriety takes effort. Is this effort not worth it, if both quality of life and survival represent the ultimate payoff?

HAVING A SENSE OF HUMOR –

As recovering alcoholics and drug addicts, we tend to take life much too seriously. For a vast majority of people with a predisposition toward depression, a pessimistic outlook on life is to be expected. Also, when alcoholics and drug addicts numb their emotions with their drugs of choice, they are also numbing positive emotions. In recovery, they have the ability to reexperience joy, happiness, love, and humor. A sense of humor is also very often a defense mechanism for those who have suffered. As a group, alcoholics and drug addicts have had more than their share of suffering and would be good candidates for developing a sense of humor.

ESTEEM AND SELF-ESTEEM –

Esteem is how we value others, and self-esteem is how we value ourselves. Alcoholics and drug addicts have a tendency to blame others for their problems. This makes it very difficult to have any esteem for others. Low self-esteem is extremely common among alcoholics and drug addicts and results from the gradual degradation of values. The addiction acts to replace any values that the alcoholic or drug addict may have had, until poor self-esteem is the only thing left.

A POSITIVE ATTITUDE –

It has long been said that attitude is everything—as long as that attitude is positive, we are in agreement. Having an open mind is essential to having a positive attitude. We must be able to leave all our perceptions, prejudices, preconceived notions, judgments, opinions, and negative attitudes behind. Positive attitudes can account for many beneficial outcomes in life. A positive attitude can also have an influence on job security, all things being equal.

RESPECT AND SELF-RESPECT –

Self-respect cannot be obtained until a moderate level of self-esteem has been attained. Since addiction is characterized by a gradual erosion of values, the chronic alcoholic or drug addict is unable to achieve respect when there is little to be respected. Also, the stigma that society places on alcoholics and drug addicts results in shame. Shame cannot lead to respect or self-respect. Frequent incarceration of alcoholics and drug addicts results in even greater shame. Over time, sobriety replaces feelings of profound shame with feelings of competence, self-confidence, pride and achievement. It is out of these ego-enhancing characteristics that self respect is born. It is from self respect and the self-nurturing that accompanies it that respect for others can emerge.

RELIGION –

I am going to define religion as a person's belief system. From our belief system we gain hope and strength. Alcoholics and drug addicts, through their addiction and the ever increasing role it plays in their lives, often alienate themselves from their core beliefs. While sobriety does not on its own restore those beliefs, it gives the alcoholic or drug addict the opportunity to return to a place that once gave them comfort.

Religion can also play an important role in reducing cravings as some alcoholics and drug addicts use prayer as a form of distraction until the craving effectively subsides.

NATURE –

Natural settings such as beaches, woods, mountains, etc. promote relaxation, which can contribute to eliminate stress and anxiety, both frequent triggers to addiction. Sports such as canoeing, kayaking, walking, and fishing all have the same effect. A caveat must be mentioned at this point, "fishing with a 12 pack of beer does very little to increase patience, let alone sobriety."

FEAR OF DEATH –

To the alcoholic or drug addict, the fear of death is very real. We are not talking about premature death and not death from natural causes. It was mentioned earlier that the human body is very resilient. It does, however, need time to recover. Chronic alcoholism and drug addiction may not allow sufficient time for full recovery. Also, what begins as a minor impairment for vital organs in the long term may become irreversible. For those alcoholics and drug addicts who are unwilling to face the consequences of their addiction, the sudden loss of addicted friends or family may be an eye-opener.

Accidents also account for many drug and alcohol-related deaths. While these are unpredictable, loss of coordination, poor balance and poor reflexes are all a predictable outcome from our addiction.

MEETINGS –

As mentioned earlier, meetings can serve many different functions in the life of the alcoholic or drug addict. The primary purpose of meetings is to create a safe environment for the alcoholic or drug addict to discuss matters that pertain to his or her addiction without the shame and stigma and judgment that society is so quick to propagate. While there are some differences in the various meetings that are available in any particular area, the fundamental purpose remains the same. Meetings can also be used to meet social needs: Whether it's to provide an opportunity to meet other recovering drug addicts or alcoholics, or refuge for those alcoholics or drug addicts who have had to take leave of their drinking or using friends and now find themselves lonely. Despite the many benefits that meetings can provide there is at least one major drawback. Any particular meeting cannot guarantee the sobriety of any of its members. If we establish a friendship with anyone we meet at a meeting and they should relapse while in our company, our sobriety now becomes at risk. Also, any particular meeting is only as good as its individual members. If you should attend a group that is not meeting your needs, it may be time to try another one. In all cases it may be helpful to take what you can use and leave the rest.

FEAR OF BEING ALONE –

Alcoholics and drug addicts, especially in early sobriety, are afraid of being alone. This amounts to a trust issue rather than a matter of social adaptability. The reasoning is based on accountability. When we are alone, we are no longer accountable to anyone else; no one will know if we are drinking or using. Wrong – we are ultimately responsible for our behavior whether in the presence of others or in the solitude of our place of residence. However, it must also be said that loneliness or any other uncomfortable emotion can be a trigger to drink or use for the alcoholic or drug addict. In short-term sobriety especially, the newly sober individual may have eliminated many friendships deemed to be negative. Meetings can play a role to fill the social void created by sobriety.

NOT BEING ABLE TO AFFORD MEDICATION –

Medication can play an important role to the sober alcoholic or drug addict. Medication can help regulate mood swings, eliminate psychosis and manage anxiety, all triggers to drink or use. Medication can also create problems when prescribed to someone who would have a tendency to abuse his or her medication. For that reason, most physicians would be best informed if they were to obtain a complete drug and alcohol history prior to prescribing medication in the opioid, benzodiazepine or sedative-hypnotic classifications. For those who are unable to afford their medication, they can work with their physician and attempt to obtain a less expensive medication, request free samples for their medication, or write to the pharmaceutical company that makes their medication to see if they have a reduced cost program for which they would be eligible. If it were drugs or alcohol that the alcoholic or drug addict could not afford, they would be extremely resourceful. This ingenuity could also be applied in obtaining their medication.

ENJOYING LIFE –

In AA literature and at AA meetings, the good life is frequently mentioned. To many alcoholics and drug addicts whose addiction has led them to depression, this is very difficult for them to imagine. How can someone who has lost faith be expected to suddenly have faith? Can poor self esteem actually lead to a good life? We are talking about extremes. The good life cannot be obtained overnight. Many alcoholics and drug addicts are impulsive. For them a long-term goal is making it to the end of the day. The good life takes effort and determination and the ability to withstand all the different bumps with which the road of life is paved. The key is that sobriety must be enjoyed. If we are unable to enjoy sobriety, then drinking and using can only be around the corner.

THE PERCEPTION THAT DRINKING AND USING WILL BE TOO HARD TO QUIT –

The fear of failure can lead to success. If we are down to our last relapse, which we are unable to determine in advance, we can only look forward to a lifetime of misery. This can act as a powerful motivator to remain on course without wandering off the path to sobriety.

GET OFF THE STRESS EXPRESS –

There are times when stress is all around us. It cannot be avoided, but it can be effectively managed. There are basically two types of stress: The stress that cannot be changed and must be accepted, and self-imposed stress that can be eliminated. What are some of the things we can do to eliminate stress? Get organized, make lists, prioritize, practice good time management. Stress, left to its own devices, represents the number one cause for relapse for both substance abuse and mental health. Many of these relapses can be avoided through stress management. Also, many physical symptoms can result from stress. Heart disease represents only one of those. The greatest factor of all in managing stress is represented by exercise.

ACCEPTANCE –

Without acceptance, the alcoholic or drug addict is doomed to a life of frustration and alienation. Relapse cannot be far behind. Acceptance can also be viewed as the surrender of denial. Acceptance allows the alcoholic or drug addict to take measures that will facilitate sobriety. While we are in denial we are unable to effectuate change. Change permits us to perceive a better life. Denial maintains the status quo that represents our addiction along with any hope for a better life.

PRIDE OVER LONG-TERM SOBRIETY –

Long-term sobriety represents a significant achievement. To achieve long-term sobriety, the many hurdles that life presents have been successfully negotiated. A minor lapse will rob us of our long-term sobriety and reset the meter to zero. The fear of having to overcome all of life's obstacles again can be enough to keep the alcoholic or drug addict focused, in order to maintain what makes us proud and not risk all that we have gained.

DREAMS –

Dreams serve a healthy function in order to provide on a subconscious level what is desired but cannot be obtained on a conscious level. What would the sober alcoholic or clean drug addict desire most? Drinking or using dreams allow sober alcoholics and drug addicts to fantasize in their sleep about drinking and using without putting their sobriety in jeopardy. Some alcoholics and drug addicts are afraid of these dreams and think that they represent predictions of drug and alcohol use in their waking hours, similar to a craving. On the contrary, a drinking or using dream should eliminate any short-term thoughts about drinking or using and should relieve any anxiety about drug or alcohol use, at least on a temporary basis.

ROMANCE –

In relationships in which there is only one alcoholic or drug addict, there is a constant state of turmoil. The non-addicted partner finds himself/herself on an emotional rollercoaster. There is such a disparity between partners that the relationship is characterized by imbalance. Intimacy, which may have previously existed, is now absent from the relationship. The addiction becomes the only matter of importance. Romancing the bottle or the drug becomes paramount. In sobriety, intimacy can flourish. Our partner becomes our significant other. We can shower them with attention and affection. Intimacy can now develop freely and lead to passion. In our addiction, our partner's role was reduced to thwart our relationship with alcohol and drugs.

PRIORITIZING SOBRIETY –

For sobriety to flourish it must become the focus of all our attention; the number one priority in our lives. Everything else becomes secondary. Without sobriety it becomes a matter of time before we have nothing. For sobriety to be successful we must want to quit more than we want to drink or use. Some alcoholics and drug addicts are ambivalent about their addiction. They know that they need to quit, but at the same time they don't want to give up what has become so familiar to them. These people will be able to enjoy periods of sobriety along with frequent lapses and relapses. Sobriety requires a commitment. Drinking and using does too. Which do you choose?

NEGATIVE CONSEQUENCES OF DRINKING OR USING –

The negative consequences of our addiction could probably come close to filling another book. Long-term alcohol and drug addiction will rob us of everything we have: Our health, our relationships, our home, our values, our families, our pride, our self esteem, our money – and even our sanity. Some of the physiological effects of alcohol and drug addiction include loss of balance, poor coordination, poor reflexes and slurred speech. Some of the physical consequences include blackouts, loss of memory, loss of brain cells, poor judgment, and seizure disorders. Legal problems can lead to frequent incarcerations and financial problems can lead to homelessness. Spiritual bankruptcy also can represent a consequence of our addiction. Is our addiction starting to lose some of its appeal?

FEAR –

To the alcoholic or drug addict who has been self medicating unpleasant emotions, fear becomes something to be dealt with in sobriety. There are basically two types of fear: Healthy fear and unhealthy fear. Healthy fear is, for the most part, instinctual. It is what causes a wild animal to run away as we approach. It is what causes us to feel anxious when a wild animal approaches us. It is what triggers the fight or flight response. Healthy fear is rational. Unhealthy fear is not. It represents a maladaptive response to a situation that may have been previously appropriate. It can also represent irrational generalizations to situations, often based on a false premise. Sobriety leads us to challenge our fears, maintain those that are vital to our survival and eliminate those whose only purpose is to cause anxiety and lead to relapse.

FEELING FREE TO DRINK NON-ALCOHOLIC BEVERAGES –

Most alcoholics gradually eliminate non-alcoholic beverages from their diet as alcohol plays a bigger role in their lives. Some alcoholics will even refuse to go to restaurants that don't serve liquor or socialize with people who do not drink like them. Sobriety represents a period of rediscovery. The recovering alcoholic is now able to reacquire a taste for those beverages that were previously imbibed and, for those who are more adventurous, may even try something new at the risk of liking it.

DESIRE TO REDISCOVER CREATIVITY –

Many creative minds succumb to alcoholism and drug addiction. The fallacy that some recreational drugs can lead to mind expanding experiences was widely believed in the drug culture of the sixties. Mind-altering, however, does not mean mind expanding. As a matter of fact, both alcohol and drug use destroy brain cells. These cells are not regenerated. How can mind expansion occur when there is actually a contraction on the cellular level? Can creativity be enhanced by drugs and alcohol or is creativity the victim of excessive indulgence?

INDEPENDENCE –

Independence implies freedom. Addiction implies dependence. Alcoholics and drug addicts will become totally consumed by their drug of choice. Lying, stealing, and manipulating are only some of the tactics they can use to obtain what they are unable to do without. Alcoholics and drug addicts long to escape from those who exert control over them. Drugs and alcohol represent a liberating experience from this resulting in their use and abuse of substances. However, they develop a false sense of priorities. It is not unusual that in early-sobriety many alcoholics or drug addicts are court ordered to take parenting classes. In sobriety we are no longer distracted from our primary role as parents. Environment also can be an important influence on children's values. If the parents become intoxicated on a regular basis, it becomes much easier for children to accept that behavior as the norm. While sober parents do not represent a guarantee that their children will grow up drug and alcohol free, addicted parents increase the likelihood of having addicted children. Not only do the children follow the example of their parents, but addicted parents also can be extremely dysfunctional. This can set the stage for future generations of alcoholics and drug addicts. When parents abuse substances it also becomes very difficult for them to tell their children to say no to drugs and alcohol. Children who get mixed messages do not always know how to act. Sobriety resolves any of this ambiguity.

DISCIPLINE –

The alcohol and the drug addict's life is full of chaos. Alcoholics and drug addicts are usually not the most responsible of people. This comes from a skewed sense of priorities. Sobriety attempts to restore priorities and put a sense of order in their lives. Most alcoholics and drug addicts are in need of structure. When we no longer abuse substances we are now able to tap into a tremendous source of energy. It is this energy that will permit us to accomplish the many things that had been neglected in our addiction. Discipline also refers to our ability to make better choices. While we are drinking and/or using, our choice is always to drink or use. In sobriety we continue to have a choice, only this time we choose to remain clean and sober.

THE FEAR OF CONSEQUENCES OF
DRINKING AND USING –

To the drug addict or alcoholic, selective perception allows them to remember the good feeling they would get from their drug of choice, while they would disregard any negative consequences of their addiction. This is called euphoric recall. It is important for the alcoholic or drug addict to put this into perspective. The negative consequences of our addiction by far outweigh any perceived benefits derived from our drug of choice. This can be best illustrated by creating a comprehensive list of negative consequences of our addiction. This can also serve as a useful tool in relapse prevention, when the alcoholic or drug addict negates any euphoric recall by reciting the negative consequences of their addiction, especially when cravings are experienced.

GOOD MENTAL HEALTH PRACTICES –

Over the past 30 years, it has been discovered in increasing numbers that individuals with mental illness self medicate their psychiatric disorders with drugs and alcohol. They experiment with various substances until they find the one that makes them feel "normal." The general guidelines are that people whose condition makes them feel down will self medicate with stimulants and people whose condition makes them feel up will self medicate with depressants. Good mental health practices include taking medication as prescribed, maintaining appointments with mental health professionals, practicing good stress management, and avoiding drugs and alcohol, which may interfere with the effectiveness of medications. Also, the ability to recognize signs and symptoms of their illness early can help avert hospitalization.

PRACTICE GOOD ANGER MANAGEMENT –

To many alcoholics and drug addicts, anger can act as a trigger to their addiction. Self-medicating feelings and emotions, particularly negative ones, represents a very common practice. If we are not taught how to deal with uncomfortable feelings and emotions, we will feel the need to escape them. Drugs and alcohol represent a good alterative as they numb out all feelings. Feelings and emotions can play an important role in our lives by bringing certain things to our attention that otherwise would have remained unknown. Also, since drugs and alcohol reduce our inhibitions, someone who is sober and angry has a much better chance to remain in control than someone who is intoxicated and *equally angry*.

PRACTICE GOOD STRESS MANAGEMENT –

Stress is the leading cause of relapse. When we are under stress we often return to old behaviors. When we consider that stress is always caused by change and that sobriety represents the greatest change in the life of the alcoholic or drug addict, we can see the enormous challenge that stress presents to someone who is, initially at least, struggling with sobriety. Some stress is beyond our control, while other forms of stress can be effectively managed or eliminated by making some changes in our lives. Procrastination puts off the inevitable but at the cost of adding stress at some future date. Developing good organizational skills can eliminate some of the chaos that the alcoholic or drug addict has been accustomed to in their addiction. Undertaking an overwhelming task can appear to be less stressful, if we break the task up into smaller, more manageable parts. Stress also happens to be the leading cause for relapse of psychiatric disorders. Since psychiatric instability can be a trigger for alcohol and drug abuse, it becomes essential, if sobriety is to succeed, that the alcoholic or drug addict adopt good mental health practices. What represents the best method for coping with stress? Exercise. This does not mean that as soon as we feel stressed we run out and exercise. Exercise can actually prevent stress from occurring or lessen the degree to which we experience it. Other techniques that can be used for effective stress management include various forms of relaxation. Since stress can cause anxiety, it stands to reason that by reducing the harmful effects of stress, we have also reduced the corresponding symptomatology of anxiety.

MENTAL CLARITY –

Mental clarity enables us to think clearly. It gives us the ability to make better decisions and use better judgment. Addiction to drugs and alcohol clouds our minds and puts us in a fog. Sobriety lifts that fog, only on a gradual basis. The addicted mind has a tendency to become lazy. Sobriety alone is not enough to put our minds in gear. This will take some effort. Effort requires energy. As we know, alcohol and drugs sap our energy. Sobriety should release enough compensatory energy to fuel the mind and allow it to overcome any deficits that drugs and alcohol may have caused.

Drugs and alcohol also cause the destruction of brain cells. These cells cannot be regenerated. Sobriety allows the brain sufficient time to adapt by creating new neural pathways to those remaining cells. This also explains why sobriety helps promote mental clarify and better thinking.

BETTER CONTROL OF EMOTIONS –

As mentioned earlier, drugs and alcohol numb our emotions. Alcoholics and drug addicts who are actively drinking and using are unable to feel intense emotions. Drugs and alcohol permit them to escape from these emotions. With sobriety they must do something that has been avoided for quite some time. They must learn to feel again. As they gain greater and greater proficiency in their ability to feel, they also gain better overall control of their emotions. Since drugs and alcohol also serve to reduce our inhibitions, sobriety will act to restore them.

THE ESTABLISHMENT OF
BETTER BOUNDARIES –

A boundary is an imaginary line that serves to delineate what is acceptable and what is unacceptable in a relationship. Personal space, for example, is defined by boundaries. Relationships also can have an influence on boundaries. We do not say things to strangers that we may say to someone close. In the workplace, employers would not be advised to make any sexual comments or innuendos to employees of the opposite sex. In this setting a breach of boundary is called sexual harassment and employers who are unable to maintain good boundaries may find themselves in legal proceedings. Parenting is another area where good boundaries must be upheld. Children need structure and boundaries help define that structure. Alcoholics and drug addicts, while they are drinking and using, typically do not have good boundaries. Poor impulse control and reduced inhibitions would severely restrict the amount of control needed for the establishment and maintenance of good boundaries. Sobriety returns the control needed for boundaries back to the individual. The desire and willingness to use good boundaries now becomes essential.

THE NEED TO PRACTICE GOOD VALUES –

Long-term alcohol and drug addiction will eventually eliminate most of the good values that are inherent in a person. Eventually, the only value left is the pursuit of our drug of choice. Lying, cheating, manipulating and stealing are all activities in which many alcoholics and drug addicts become willing participants. These activities, in turn, contribute to the low self-esteem that is pervasive in this population. As the alcoholic or drug addict begins his recovery, he also begins to rediscover those values that had been alienated by his addiction. Self-esteem begins to recover and a sense of pride replaces any previous feelings of shame.

SAFE SEX PRACTICES –

Addiction to drugs and alcohol promotes risky, promiscuous sexual behavior. As mentioned earlier, alcohol increases impulsivity and reduces inhibitions. This leads to an increase in sexual partners and greater risk in contracting AIDS or a number of other, less deadly but equally harmful diseases. Does sobriety automatically imply safe sex? No, but it gives those recovering alcoholics and drug addicts who would like to adopt these practices the ability to do so. Safe sex always represents a choice. Sobriety increases our ability to make good choices. When we have better control of our impulses and our inhibitions are once again restored, the risks attached to promiscuous sexual activity should be effectively reduced.

THE VITAL ROLE OF INHIBITIONS –

Inhibitions play a protective role. Inhibitions can, at times, counteract impulsive behavior. Inhibitions can act to reduce or eliminate promiscuous behavior, while drugs and alcohol can accelerate it. Inhibitions also can filter out inappropriate comments that would otherwise have negative consequences. They can prevent us from saying something rude to our boss or something hurtful to our significant other. Drugs and alcohol act to remove that filter and face the consequences of being uninhibited. Alcohol has often been called a social lubricant and has the effect of loosening up someone who is otherwise considered "uptight." This liberating experience, however, comes at a price. Alcoholics often find themselves having to apologize for comments that they made that they later regretted. This is assuming that they have any recollection at all of what they said in the first place.

DIET AND NUTRITION –

Alcoholics and drug addicts typically have many nutritional deficits. This is in part due to the fact that many alcoholics and drug addicts substitute drugs and/or alcohol for food. Alcohol will also cause malabsorption of nutrients causing some deficits of the very same nutrients that they are consuming. It is also important for alcoholics to avoid refined sugar and caffeine as they may increase cravings. The popularity of caffeine for many alcoholics must be seriously reconsidered here. B vitamins represent the most common group of vitamins that the alcoholic would typically need. Thiamine (B1) would be the most common. Thiamine can be found in asparagus, mushrooms, peanuts, pork, soybeans, sunflower seeds and yeast. Whole wheat and nuts also contain a good amount of thiamine. Also recommended would be a high potency vitamin and mineral supplement and a B-vitamin complex as first step nutritional supplements.

SERENITY –

Serenity is the ability to be at peace with ourselves and those around us. The fast pace of everyday life has left many of us wanting more peace and quiet. For some this can only be obtained by rising long before the rest of society. This, of course, would require an early bedtime at night. For the recovering alcoholic or drug addict who used to abuse substances well into the night, a substantial portion of their drinking and using would now be replaced by sleep. For some alcoholics or drug addicts, sleep represents the only time of the day or night when they did not drink or use. In some ways, serenity represents the equivalent of sleep only in our waking hours. When we are serene we do not have a need for drugs or alcohol. How do we achieve serenity? Meditation, various forms of relaxation and spirituality are all methods, that, when practiced regularly, can promote and enhance serenity.

COMPETENCE –

Competence is the ability to assimilate expertise in a certain area. Competence is usually measured in comparison to others who are performing the same duties or tasks as we are. Competence, quantitatively, can be measured by performance evaluations, customer satisfaction surveys, quotas or piecemeal production. Due to the progressive nature of drug and alcohol addiction, competence for the alcoholic and drug addict, for the most part, should be on the decline over time. Absenteeism and poor job performance are usually pretty characteristic of the alcoholic or drug-addicted employee. In recovery, the alcoholic or drug addict should be better able to perform. Good work habits must, however, be instilled since both alcohol and drug addiction have probably left these lacking. Some alcoholics and drug addicts may even excel out of a strong desire to prove their ability to be equal or even superior to their non-addicted coworkers.

REALISTIC EXPECTATIONS –

Having realistic expectations will contribute to reducing our overall level of frustration. High levels of frustration can lead to self-medicating with alcohol and/or drugs. Unrealistic expectations will increase our levels of frustration along with our potential for relapse. Some individuals are much more able to tolerate frustration than others. Impulsivity does not usually lead to high levels of frustration tolerance. The ability to handle stress well would generally indicate good potential for handling frustration well. Recognizing the difference between whether we can have an influence on change or whether change cannot be influenced and must be accepted will also have a considerable influence on our overall level of frustration. Having realistic expectations, however, does not mean that we cannot dream or fantasize as long as we are aware that these dreams and fantasies represent an escape from reality that may at times even be necessary.

GOOD SLEEP HABITS –

Drugs and alcohol will either prevent restful sleep or result in the complete inability to sleep. Sleep disturbances can occur for up to two years during sobriety depending on the individual and their drug and alcohol history. All drugs in the stimulant category will prevent sleep. This includes caffeine. Alcohol, when it is consumed in sufficient quantities, will actually promote sleep, albeit temporarily, when the alcohol begins to wear off, so does its soporific effects. The alcoholic then has a choice to consume more alcohol in order to promote sedation or wait for sleep to occur naturally. When alcoholics feel that they are not able to sleep without a "nightcap" they end up in a cycle that can be very difficult to break out of. In sobriety, good sleep habits are gradually restored until the recovering alcoholic can sleep restfully and naturally without resorting to sedating substances. The best sleep aid of all remains physical and mental exertion that results in fatigue.

BEING FLEXIBLE –

Being flexible allows us to adapt to certain situations. It is also a good indicator of good stress management. When we are flexible we are not as susceptible to stress. Alcoholics and drug addicts can be very rigid. Sobriety requires flexibility. When recovering alcoholics and drug addicts face an obstacle in their sobriety, a flexible approach becomes necessary. Sometimes creativity must be invoked as a response to frustrating people or situations. Having an open mind can also allow us to be flexible. We are able to consider and at times even accept new approaches to doing things without automatically rejecting them. Flexibility also includes a willingness to try new activities that may enhance and broaden our sobriety base.

BEING RIGID –

This may appear to be contradictory with the previous paragraph but sobriety really requires a combination of flexibility and rigidity. A rigid approach to sobriety is not all encompassing. Discipline in our lives as well as our sobriety will serve the recovering alcoholic or drug addict well. The discipline of consistently saying no to drugs and alcohol will prevent the recovering drug addict or alcoholic from relapsing. To the alcoholic or drug addict, the predictability and consistency of the effects of his/her drug of choice represent some of the positive reinforcements of his/her addiction. In sobriety, it becomes the consequences and negative factors associated with their drug of choice that represent the more complete picture of some of the more nefarious elements of their addiction. The chaotic lives of alcoholics and drug addicts will very often require structure. This brings an element of stability in their lives and can make their lives more manageable. Any attempt at control must be abandoned. Controlling behavior will often result in a trigger to drink or use and will only result in resentment. As the recovering alcoholic or drug addict is able to gain more self control in sobriety, the need for control is replaced by an increasing need for assertiveness and independence – independence from his/her addiction as well as independence in his/her relationships. The imbalance that was previously the result of the addiction is now replaced by another imbalance resulting from sobriety and a desire for independence. It is not only the addiction that puts stress on a relationship, but sobriety can also have the same effect.

BEING ORGANIZED –

Good organizational skills can simplify our lives a great deal. We are living in a world that is becoming increasingly more complex. Technological advances are occurring at a rapid pace. The expectation to keep up just adds to our preexisting stress load. Being organized in our lives as well as the workplace better prepares us for the inevitable: STRESS. Not only is our ability to handle stress enhanced by our organizational skills but we feel more in control of our lives. This translates into a greater feeling of confidence in our work as well as a more positive attitude derived from not feeling overwhelmed all the time. Being organized can also help us avoid feeling "burned out." When we are organized we become more efficient and more productive. When we spend less time looking for things, we have more time to spend on our work. We are also better able to keep track of appointments, deadlines, phone calls, and anything else that is required and essential to the efficient operation of the workplace.

KNOWING YOUR LIMITATIONS –

Sobriety is a learning process. As our sobriety gains strength over time, our ability to handle certain situations increases. It is important that we learn to discern what we are capable of and what remains "slippery ground." In early sobriety we are going through uncharted waters. We must deal with situations sober for the first time. This includes going to weddings or other events where alcohol is served and consumption is encouraged, attending a Super Bowl Party, or just getting together with a friend that we used to drink or use with without knowing how he/she would react to our newly-acquired sober lifestyle. In general should we have any doubt at all about our ability to deal with a particular situation without jeopardizing our sobriety, that situation should be avoided until such time when we have gained enough confidence and strength in our sobriety. Knowing your limitations would also include recognizing lapses and relapses as potential learning tools from which we can prevent any lapses or relapses from occurring in the future.

Many recovering alcoholics and drug addicts, after an initial period of sobriety (usually three to four months), become over-confident and ignore the reality of their limitations. This is why, other than the initial stages of sobriety, the three to four month period of sobriety represents the most common period of relapse. For that reason, it is important that when certain sobriety dates are celebrated we also reinforce the fact that many challenges lie ahead of us if we want to continue to keep our sobriety intact.

KNOWING YOUR STRENGTHS –

As we progress in our recovery we must recognize that our sobriety gives us the increasing ability to handle situations that had been previously avoided. We should also feel the need to attend less support groups as in the past. If the purpose of sobriety is to gradually reintegrate the individual back into society, then the support group meeting should begin to play a lesser role in the life of the recovering alcoholic or drug addict. Someone who has been sober for five years should not be attending 20 meetings a week. Either they lack enough self-confidence to break away on their own or else they have now become addicted to their meetings. To tell an individual how many meetings are appropriate for their recovery would go beyond the scope of this book, but it stands to reason that as sobriety increases, the need for meetings is diminished. Knowing your strengths allows us to gauge whether the number of meetings is appropriate to the corresponding level of sobriety. To know your strength also means being able to determine whether we are now able to attempt something that had previously been avoided without putting our sobriety at risk.

EATING REGULARLY –

To alcoholics and drug addicts, their priorities are very often skewed towards obtaining, drinking, or using their drug of choice. Eating becomes secondary. In sobriety, structure ensures that meals will be eaten at regular times. Nutrients can now be absorbed since alcohol will not longer be interfering. Alcohol will also not cause the alcoholic to forget meals since he/she is now in recovery.

ABILITY TO BE MORE ALERT –

Since alcohol is a depressant that can also have a sedating effect, sobriety will cause an immediate increase in alertness. This includes mental acuity, reflexes, balance, memory retrieval, agility, and coordination. These factors will translate into an immediate improvement in performance related to driving skills, as well as job-related skills. An overall potential for less accidents both inside and outside the workplace can also be a direct consequence of being more alert.

ABILITY TO MAINTAIN BETTER COORDINATION –

Alcohol deadens reflexes. Our reaction time is increased in direct proportion to the amount we drink. Although we have the illusion of being able to handle it, this stems from a false sense of reality that alcohol can provide by decreasing our ability to have good judgment. A good test on the impact that alcohol has on coordination is the field sobriety test which can help determine if the individual is sufficiently impaired to present a danger to the general public. Poor coordination has caused some alcoholics to raise their drink in the general vicinity of their face and miss their mouth. Other alcoholics are unable to eat their meals without spilling their food all over themselves or around their plate. This is the result of poor hand-eye coordination. Any type of endeavor that requires a keen sense of agility is going to require intense concentration and superior coordination. Imagine a juggling act in which one or both performers is impaired by alcohol.

ABILITY TO MAINTAIN BALANCE –

Some of the symptoms of alcohol that will cause sedation are also responsible for loss of balance. This, in turn, is responsible for the many accidents that result from intoxication. Alcohol is one of the leading causes of accidents in this country. I even know of a case where someone who had been drinking excessively fell into a campfire. Not only was he unable to save himself but the injuries he suffered were aggravated by his friends' slower reaction time. They were drinking, too!

ABILITY TO AVOID ACCIDENTS –

Reflexes are directly impaired in proportion to the amount of alcohol consumed. Reaction time, alertness, and hand-eye coordination must all be in the normal to superior range if the sudden apparition of a car in our field of vision is to be avoided. Accidents can and do occur without any intoxication involved. Alcohol only compounds the problem. Fires are also frequently caused by people under the influence of alcohol or drugs, smoking in bed and falling asleep. Many innocent people are often killed in these fires. As previously mentioned, many other accidents around the house and in the workplace result from impaired functioning associated with alcohol consumption.

ABILITY TO MAINTAIN DRIVING PRIVILEGES –

Driving under the influence of alcohol or other psychoactive substances is against the law. While the blood/alcohol level (BAL) varies from state to state, there is, generally speaking, very little tolerance for driving under the influence. Usually, the first DUI can be considered an error in judgment while the second one is almost always considered an indication of a more serious problem. Driving privileges can already be suspended on the first violation. The severity of the suspension varies along with the seriousness and frequency of the violation. Some licenses can be restricted; some can be suspended, while others can be revoked. In the past, it was possible to get a license revoked in one state, apply for a new one in another and drive for many years without arousing any suspicion. Now, with the widespread use of computers in most law enforcement cruisers, driving records can be verified and multi-state offenders arrested. Driving privileges can be subsequently withheld or revoked.

ABILITY TO MAINTAIN CONTROL –

Alcoholics and drug addicts have very often experienced a rigid, controlling environment in their family of origin. For that reason, when they experiment with drugs and alcohol, the sensation of being out of control represents a liberating experience that is going to be replicated time and time again. What the alcoholic or drug addict fails to realize is that in the process of escaping from parental control, the alcoholic or drug addict now finds himself/herself under the control of an addictive substance, very often a much more difficult type of control than the original one from which he or she sought to escape. Sobriety gives us the ability to regain control – control of our speech, control of our emotions, control of ourselves. Violent acts such as domestic violence, rape, and sexual abuse can be averted with better control. A lower incidence of verbal abuse and promiscuity can also be expected when we are more in control. Being in better control will also result in fewer traffic accidents along with a decrease in fatalities.

ABILITY TO MAINTAIN ENERGY –

Since alcohol causes malabsorption of nutrients, energy levels in alcoholics become rapidly depleted. Since alcohol is also known to cause depression, one of the most common symptoms of depression is lack of energy. This may also be the reason most alcoholics have a very strong tendency to procrastinate. In recovery, improved nutrition and the establishment of an exercise program will result in a substantial increase in energy. Bad habits related to the addiction would still need to be overcome, however, for the full benefit of increased energy levels to be maintained.

ABILITY TO MAINTAIN MOTIVATION –

Alcoholics and drug addicts have a tendency to be apathetic. As the progression of their addiction continues to deteriorate, they tend to lose interest in activities that they previously felt pleasurable. This is partially due to the fact that their addiction has taken a priority over everything else in their lives. Also, as depression begins to manifest itself, the alcoholic or drug addict may suffer from anhedonia, a fairly common symptom related to their loss or interest in all that is pleasurable. This, in turn, is related to a decrease in libido, a condition that is aggravated by most anti-depressant medications. As sobriety is achieved over time, the alcoholic or drug addict will experience a gradual return to motivation, assuming that his/her mood will have stabilized either on its own or through the assistance of medication.

BETTER CONTROL OF IMPULSES –

In all addictions there is a greater tendency towards impulsivity. This is due, in part, to the role drugs and alcohol play in reducing our inhibitions. Also, cravings are very often interpreted as a supreme command that we must absolutely drink or use while, in reality, cravings are fleeting and will eventually disappear on their own, given enough time. In sobriety, the alcoholic or drug addict will eventually learn how to handle cravings effectively. Also, the introduction of thought should help control addictive impulses. Many alcoholics and drug addicts are highly intelligent people who, while under the influence, need some assistance in making good decisions.

NEED TO ELIMINATE MONEY AS A TRIGGER TO DRINK OR USE –

To the alcoholic or drug addict, money very often has taken on a new meaning. It represents the gateway to their addiction. Without money the alcoholic or drug addict must resort to stealing, shoplifting, or pawning merchandise in order to obtain their drug of choice. If the alcoholic or drug addict is employed, payday represents an opportunity to drink or use often at the expense of such necessities as food or paying the rent or mortgage. For those alcoholics or drug addicts whose employers offer direct deposit for their wages, this gives them the opportunity to eliminate some of the temptation associated with handling money. For others, having a trusted friend or relative (not another alcoholic or drug addict) distribute money to them as needed may also help remove some of the opportunity for impulsivity. As sobriety eventually progresses to the point where the individual no longer is in need of such close financial monitoring, his/her need for independence can once again assert itself.

GOOD WEATHER –

Weather can have an important influence on mood. Seasonal Affective Disorder results when individuals who live in climates where there is not enough sunlight develop a form of depression. Also, people who work nights and sleep days can be prone to this disorder. The tendency for individuals who are depressed to self-medicate with dugs and alcohol is well known. In Scandinavia, which has a very high incidence of both suicide and alcoholism, the fact that they have very few hours of daylight in winter is not coincidental. The need to frequently be indoors will also contribute to an increase in both alcohol and drug consumption. To those who are able, relocating to a climate that is more favorable can represent a solution.

TRUSTING ONESELF AND OTHERS –

Drug and alcohol addictions have a component that is extremely irrational. The alcoholic or drug addict will experience an internal dialogue between the sober, rational mind and the irrational addicted mind. In early sobriety the alcoholic or drug addict will tend to be more receptive to the addicted mind. As sobriety progresses, the sober mind will exert a greater influence on the individual who is now able to make better decisions. Trusting oneself also involves making sober choices, which in the past may have led to relapse. Trusting others often involves taking small risks at first followed by greater and greater risks as the level of trust increases.

ELIMINATING ANY CROSS ADDICTIONS –

Many alcoholics and drug addicts develop addictions to substances other than their drug of choice. These substances serve a similar purpose to the alcoholic or drug addict – a temporary escape from reality. Should they decide to give up their drug of choice and not the other substances in their lives, there is a very good likelihood that, given enough time, they will return to their primary addiction. Since all addictions are irrational, if the alcoholic or drug addict can rationalize using one substance they should also be able to rationalize a return to their drug of choice. Being irrational does not necessarily mean our behavior must be inconsistent. Also, while we maintain any cross addictions, the addictive mind continues to be nurtured at the expense of the sober mind. Eventually, the addictive mind will overtake the sober mind and start longing for our drug of choice. This will lead to cravings and eventually relapse.

PLANNING FUN DAYS –

To the recovering alcoholic and drug addict in early sobriety, fun is a relatively new concept. When we spend years numbing our emotions we can become somewhat disoriented in society. Fun can be viewed as one of the keys to sobriety. If we are unable to have fun, the addicted mind can come out of hibernation and make its demands known. Since many recovering alcoholics and drug addicts are also suffering from depression, they have difficulty even understanding how to go about having fun. At first it may be necessary to set some time aside every week to enjoy fun activities. Thee activities must first be given some thought. For those who have difficulty determining what may be fun, a useful tip would be to think back to childhood. What was enjoyable back then could very well still be enjoyable now.

SELF-AWARENESS –

Introspection, or the ability to look within, represents a major element related to self-awareness. Self-awareness allows us to look at ourselves objectively. It will also allow the recovering alcoholic or drug addict to analyze whether denial is accurate or an irrational means to protect the addiction. Self-awareness can also be referred to as the spiritual awakening in Alcoholics Anonymous, when the alcoholic or drug addict has a brief moment of lucidity in which their addiction is actually put into question. Is my drinking or using considered normal? Do other people drink or use like me? Has my quality of life improved since I began using alcohol or drugs? How much of my misfortune can be attributed to alcohol, drugs, or just bad luck? These questions and many others help establish a foundation from which sobriety can be built. Without self-awareness, we remain in the dark. We allow our addiction to control us and direct our lives. It is only in sobriety that we are able to reestablish our destiny and influence the course that our lives will take.

INSIGHT –

Insight represents the ability to take mere observations and draw conclusions. For close to 20 years I was aware that I had not been hired following a job interview. Only 20 years later, in sobriety, did I realize that there might have been a connection between not being hired and the scotch whiskey on my breath. In our addiction events occur independently of one another. They are not part of our self-awareness. In sobriety we begin to make connections. We see the cause and effect of our behavior. This is what is meant by insight. In sobriety we begin to see the predictive nature of our addiction. If I go to a bar or a crack house, I will most probably drink or use. If I stop taking my antidepressants, I will find another way to control my mood. It is this ability to draw logical conclusions from our behavior that will allow us to maintain and broaden our sobriety.

GOALS AND HOPE –

Without goals we tend to stagnate. Goals keep us moving forward. Goals must be realistic for them to be achievable. If goals are unrealistic they become a constant source of frustration. For that reason we must be flexible when we establish our goals. When our goals are achieved, we exhibit a sense of self-satisfaction, a sense of pride. This leads to greater self-esteem. Hope is what keeps us alive. Even if we are experiencing major disappointments and setbacks in our lives, hope gives us the ability to look beyond the present and into the future, while maintaining a positive outlook. In a lot of ways, hope represents the antithesis of anxiety. When someone loses hope he or she is at risk for severe depression and even suicide. Hope can often be restored through the discovery of what motivates the person to stay alive and how suicide will not present an effective solution to their problems.

ENJOYING EVERY MOMENT OF LIFE TO THE FULLEST (BUT RESPONSIBLY) –

Life can be unpredictable. So is death. Without getting into a discussion of the afterlife or reincarnation, which goes beyond the scope of this book, we have a responsibility to ourselves to live life as if tomorrow will be our last day … it might be. To the recovering alcoholic and addict, this means that we must maintain and even surpass the quality of life that sobriety has given us. Happiness really is a choice, but for happiness to occur certain conditions must be met. How can we be happy if we are surrounded by negativity? A conscious effort must be made to eliminate all those negative factors that prevent us from being happy. Some of these negative factors include addictions, mental illness, relationships and unsatisfying employment situations. When all these negative factors have been eliminated, will happiness then be guaranteed? Even in the best of circumstances, happiness will require effort. To live responsibly still requires completing chores, dealing with difficult people, paying bills and disciplining our children when necessary. Even these less than desirable tasks can provide happiness. The knowledge of having completed a task that we dreaded can leave a smile on our face. Our childrearing practices, including punishment and discipline, can lead to satisfaction when we see the positive results in our children. For us to be happy, we must discover what makes us happy and incorporate as many of these factors into our lives in the amount of time available. For some people this means that these activities must be scheduled into their lives. If not they are likely to get lost in the busy lives that they are leading. For others who may not have the discipline to change, it forces them to incorporate these positive changes into their lives. For those people with low self-esteem, they might not feel worthy of engaging in pleasurable activities. What better way to make someone start feeling good about themselves than by participating in an activity that is enjoyable and also gives them satisfaction.

ABILITY TO HANDLE CRAVINGS –

In early sobriety cravings are more frequent and more intense. As we become more successful in handling cravings both the frequency and intensity will subside until, eventually, they are no longer experienced. This usually will occur in mid to long-term sobriety. If, at any time in our sobriety, we should have a lapse or relapse, cravings will return. This is part of the addictive process. Cravings for drugs and alcohol will not last for more than 20 minutes. The fact that they are time limited gives us hope that a relapse is not inevitable. Cravings are like feelings – they come and they go. Even if a craving feels like a command that we must absolutely drink or use, what would be the consequences if we did not? Absolutely nothing. The only real consequence of not giving into the craving is that our sobriety would remain intact and that maybe we will have gained some confidence in our ability to handle cravings. Most methods used to handle cravings effectively involve distraction. This includes getting involved in some kind of physical activity, reading, watching TV, listening to music, meditating, praying or anything that will preoccupy the mind from thoughts of drinking or using.

GOOD HEALTH –

Illness can be very stressful. Not only do we feel bad but we may miss work, not get paid, develop financial problems and be unable to take care of chores or tasks that tend to be left undone until we are well. This leads to stress in the future. As mentioned earlier, stress is the leading cause of relapse for substance abuse and mental illness. While we are drinking and using we tend to neglect our health. After all, it costs money to be healthy. Given limited financial resources, which would an alcoholic or drug addict prefer? Spending money on their health or on their drug of choice?

Mental health can also be just as important as physical health to the recovering alcoholic or drug addict. Since in order to achieve balance and psychiatric stability we tend to self medicate with various substances, the right medication can eliminate this need and play a big role in any subsequent attempt at sobriety.

Any use of opiates in order to treat pain must be carefully monitored and prescribed judiciously since the tendency to abuse these as well as other potentially additive medications will always be a temptation to the recovering alcoholic and drug addict. When possible, prescribing addictive medications is to be avoided. However, alcoholics and drug addicts should not have to suffer more than anyone else. Their addiction alone is responsible for enough suffering. Prescriptions can be limited in quantity and refills can be restricted. Even with such careful monitoring, the possibility of supplementing prescribed medication by buying it on the street cannot be ignored.

ULTIMATUMS –

While ultimatums incorporate an element of control that most alcoholics and drug addicts find distasteful, the strategy can be effective in some cases. This would depend mainly on how well motivated the alcoholic or drug addict may be. It also forces the alcoholic or drug addict to make a choice. As alcoholics and drug addicts, we do not like to make choices. We want it all. Part of this may be human nature while part of it may be an ongoing desire to protect and maintain our addiction. An ultimatum forces us to look at the reality of the situation. We can't have it all so what do we choose – addiction or sobriety?

TO BE A GOOD ROLE MODEL FOR OUR CHILDREN –

If we, as clean and sober individuals remain drug and alcohol free, will that ensure that our children will not fall into the same trap we did? The only ones that we can keep clean and sober are ourselves. As parents, we are able to exert an influence over our children. That influence can even be a positive one. For us to tell our children to just say no to drugs, while we smoke pot in front of them or leave drug paraphernalia scattered around the house for them to find gives them mixed messages. Children do not buy into hypocrisy. If Mom and Dad are clean and sober there is a strong likelihood that their children will be, too. Parents cannot, however, shelter their children from bad influences, but as clean and sober individuals it will be much easier to point out the negative impact drugs and alcohol will have on their children's lives, if they are not drinking and using themselves. It would be nice if more celebrities who have recovered from drug and alcohol addiction would get the message out to kids about the impact their addiction has had on their lives. However, the stigma attached to drug and alcohol addiction seems to prevail in keeping their recovery low-key.

OBSERVING THE ADDICTED
BEHAVIOR OF OTHERS –

Watching behavioral changes in other people can be an amusing pastime for the recovering alcoholic or drug addict. It is important that we make the connection between their behavior and our previous behavior. While this alone may not represent a disincentive to drug or alcohol use, it can still provide a useful tool for sobriety. Going to a restaurant and observing how much other people drink and the gradual increase in the volume of their speech is a good example. Also, in order to reinforce our own sobriety, we can observe how many people in our direct vicinity in a restaurant drink non-alcoholic beverages. This helps refute the belief shared by many newly sober alcoholics that "everyone drinks." It also serves the purpose of making the newly sober alcoholic more comfortable about his or her status as a non-drinker.

RESPONSIBILITY –

Does sobriety automatically lead to responsibility? Not necessarily. Some people just have a natural ability to be irresponsible. For some individuals, though, sobriety can have a direct influence on responsible behavior. We discussed earlier how drinking and using will change the order of priorities in life. When drinking and using become our greatest priority, we tend to abandon all sense of responsibility. Bills don't get paid, cars get repossessed, and even children and pets might not get fed. Drugs and alcohol destroy neuro-chemicals in our brain. This, in part, will cause memory loss. It is this progressive loss of memory that is also one of the main factors in becoming irresponsible as a result of our drug or alcohol addiction.

ANTABUSE –

For those alcoholics who are unable to stop drinking without some additional help, Antabuse may be the answer. Antabuse is a medication that is taken daily and causes a chemical reaction when alcohol is introduced into the body. When alcoholics drink on Antabuse they become violently ill. This should act as a strong disincentive not to drink again. In many cases the disincentive is not to take the Antabuse again. Along the same line, an alcoholic who is taking Antabuse is able to plan a relapse by discontinuing the Antabuse just before the planned relapse, making sure that all the Antabuse is no longer in his or her body before the planned time to drink. Antabuse can be used as a crutch for alcoholics who are unable or unwilling to quit on their own. For others who have already experienced numerous treatment episodes without success, it can buy them enough time to make quitting more realistic. As with all medications, Antabuse should be used as prescribed and as intended and not misused.

COOKING –

To the alcoholic or drug addict, cooking often means opening a can or putting something in the microwave. Cooking accidents such as burns are often caused by poor reflexes and delayed reaction time associated with the consumption of alcohol. For some, cooking can be relaxing. The art of preparing a good meal requires a certain amount of concentration. The ability to block out all distractions and remain focused can be interpreted as a form of relaxation. For the recovering alcoholic, there is some controversy regarding cooking. Would cooking with alcohol be an acceptable practice for a recovering alcoholic? Even though the alcohol tends to burn off while it is being cooked, will the alcohol that is not used and remains in the bottle remain as a temptation to be consumed at a later date?

WORK –

Work provides us with an opportunity to earn a living. What we do with that living depends on us. Do we use the money we earn to provide for our loved ones or do we instead divert our salary or wages into drugs or alcohol? Do we spend our money wisely to enhance our quality of life or do we choose to waste it on our addiction instead? Alcoholics and drug addicts suffer from many losses throughout their lives, but their jobs are very often the last to go. Work represents a major source of income without which the alcoholic or drug addict would need to borrow or steal to finance their addiction. Through our work we can derive positive self-esteem, self confidence, pride, satisfaction, and feelings of accomplishment. Work also serves a social function as many alcoholics or drug addicts, who tend to isolate themselves, must rely on coworkers and superiors in the workplace for their limited social life.

CROSSWORD PUZZLES –

The role of crossword puzzles is twofold. Crossword puzzles can effectively distract the mind from cravings that can be persistent, intense, and relentless. They can also serve as an important aid in order to restore memory. As mentioned earlier, drugs and alcohol destroy brain cells. While these brain cells do not regenerate, sobriety will allow the brain to create new neuro-pathways by rerouting existing cells that were previously unused. Crossword puzzles will promote the formation of new connections that will strengthen the imprint on existing pathways and facilitate the retrieval of previously stored material.

NOT DRINKING OR USING –

There is nothing like stating the obvious. Refraining from drinking or using is one of the basic tenets of sobriety. At this juncture, the difference between abstaining from drugs and alcohol and sobriety must be made. The mere act of abstention, in most cases, is in itself not enough to maintain long-term sobriety. Without some of the coping skills mentioned in this book, it is just a matter of time before the addicted mind will take over and begin to dominate the sober mind. If we are able to succeed in our sobriety, we must learn to silence the addicted mind and begin to practice sobriety in all areas of our lives. Abstention is but a small microcosm of sobriety. It does, however, have a major significance in that it represents a big step towards sobriety and away from denial.

DESIRE TO GAIN OR REGAIN FREEDOM –

Addiction to drugs and/or alcohol can exert a tremendous amount of control on the alcoholic or drug addict. Escape from control is what was very often responsible for the addiction in the first place, only at first the control was psychological. Now it is both psychological and physiological. When denial is broken and replaced by early sobriety, the awareness of this control is at its strongest and is eventually replaced by a strong desire for freedom. This sense of freedom tends to grow as sobriety progresses. While freedom in general is a relative concept, it cannot coexist with any addiction that is being actively practiced.

THE THOUGHT OF HAVING TO
GO TO REHAB AGAIN –

Drug and alcohol treatment centers frequently leave bad memories with the population that they serve. The environment can be very stressful for a number of reasons: The alcoholic or drug addict finds him or herself in an unfamiliar environment; they must now face rules for the very first time since they began drinking and using; they are unable to see family unless it is during visiting hours, and some may be in a lot of physical pain. As they move further and further away from their last drink or drug, their emotions may come to the surface and emotional pain follows close behind. Finally they no longer have the security of knowing that, if they should change their minds, not only are they unable to leave but they also will no longer have access to their drug of choice during the duration of their stay. Much of this negativity results from anxiety related to the loss of their addiction and the fear of the unknown that is represented by sobriety. For those whose treatment turns out to be successful, their attitude can be very positive as they describe their experience in treatment with gratitude and praise. This, in turn, can even lead to referrals for friends and family who may be in need of such an experience. Treatment may even be the beginning of sober friendships.

PHONE LIST –

This usually refers to a list of members and their phone numbers who participate in a sobriety group on a regular basis, particularly members of SOS (Secular Organization For Sobriety). These phone lists are made available to other members as a resource to be used for relapse prevention purposes. Participation in the phone list is voluntary. Some group members may hesitate at first to give out their phone numbers to what they consider "strangers." This should be acceptable to the group.

As participation progresses over time, the original skepticism should decrease and be replaced with a willingness to share their phone number with other group members. If this does not occur, then maybe another group should be considered.

ABILITY TO MAINTAIN GOOD REFLEXES –

Since alcohol's major effect is on the brain and the brain acts to control everything that we do, it stands to reason that reflexes are going to become progressively more impaired as we continue to drink. This will result in a greater likelihood for accidents both in and out of the house. Our ability to drive can, at times, require split second decisions followed by instantaneous response times. The speed at which we respond can determine whether we live or die. In most circumstances the alcoholic can get by without experiencing extreme driving conditions. But are we able to predict in advance what lies ahead when we turn the key to the ignition?

THE REALIZATION OF THE
SERIOUSNESS OF THE PROBLEM –

To the alcoholic or drug addict who has been in denial for many years there comes a day of reckoning (or would wreckoning be more appropriate). In AA and NA they call this a spiritual awakening. It is when reality finally sets in – hitting bottom, to borrow more of the AA and NA terminology, can often trigger this realization. Some examples include finding out that our addiction has done irreversible damage to one or more of our vital organs and that our time to live has been severely compromised; that our drinking or using has caused irreparable damage to our marriage and that divorce is imminent; that our employment for which we were once valued is about to terminate as a direct result of our addiction. These represent only some of the many different situations that our addiction can have an impact on our lives and convert long-term doubters into true believers.

LETTING GO OF RESENTMENTS –

Maintaining resentment can be toxic. While forgiving and forgetting might at times be difficult, forgiving alone can be more feasible. The purpose of resentment is to serve as a reminder that someone has acted poorly towards us and, in order not to give them another opportunity to do so, we harbor ill feelings towards them as a reminder of their transgression. Forgiving and not forgetting will serve the same purpose only without the toxicity of resentment. Also, if we should find forgiveness difficult to come by, it can represent a liberating feeling that can be worth experiencing. Even when we forgive someone it does not mean that we should not proceed with caution and, depending on their response, be able to reassess the relationship and how we feel towards that person. Typical resentments of the alcoholic and drug addict will usually involve friends or family members who try to stop the alcoholic or drug addict from drinking or using, as well as anyone directly involved in their involuntary commitment to treatment. This particular resentment can take many years to get over; sometimes long after sobriety has been achieved and denial is no longer a factor.

AGE RELATED LOSS OF TOLERANCE –

As we get older, many of us find a need for different types of medication, some of which do not mix with alcohol. Medications for anxiety, pain medications and most sedative-hypnotic medications fall into this category. Also, as we age we experience a reverse tolerance for alcohol. When we mix alcohol with medications that are contraindicated, the effects of the alcohol are magnified. This is called potentiation. With our age related decreased tolerance to alcohol, the result can be catastrophic.

ABILITY TO CELEBRATE HOLIDAYS
WITHOUT DRUGS AND ALCOHOL –

We mentioned earlier that the alcoholic and drug addict suffers many losses in early sobriety. Celebrating holidays without alcohol or drugs can represent a major challenge. On holidays people who usually don't drink will indulge. What is the recovering alcoholic to do? Stay home and hide in a closet? One strategy that can help minimize the importance of "drinking holidays" is to volunteer to work on those days. Since many workplaces are closed on these holidays, it is always possible to get together with other recovering alcoholics and drug addicts and celebrate the holiday in a sober fashion. It is also recommended that we celebrate our sobriety date with friends or family in order to help offset those celebrations that we choose not to participate in because of our desire, at first, not to be in a drinking environment. Other than holidays, there are many other occasions that the newly sober alcoholic should seriously consider whether to attend, i.e., weddings, Super Bowl parties, after work get-togethers with fellow employees as well as any particular activity that has a strong link to drinking, such as fishing or even bowling, for some.

ABILITY TO MAKE BETTER DECISIONS –

While we are under the influence, our judgment becomes impaired. Drugs and alcohol can lead us to believe that we are able to do just about anything. Alcohol is also called "liquid courage." Both alcohol and drugs can make us take leave of our senses. How often do friends or relatives give us an accurate description of our behavior the day after we overindulged only to be met with disbelief and incredulity. Sobriety does not protect us from poor judgment and bad decisions, but it gives us the opportunity to use our judgment and make decisions without the mental fog that drugs and alcohol can create. Why should we incapacitate our ability to reason, our memory, or our mental process just for a few moments of feeling high? Drugs and alcohol represent an escape from reality, but what about those issues that must absolutely be dealt with while our brain is on vacation?

ABILITY TO MAINTAIN JOB PERFORMANCE AT A HIGH LEVEL –

Substance abuse can affect job performance at many different levels. High rates of absenteeism, poor job performance, and increased number of accidents on the job are all related to substance abuse. Absenteeism can be attributed to recovering from substance abuse and can be difficult to measure as alcoholics and drug addicts will tend to call in sick without specifying the nature of their illness. Not surprising, Mondays are the most frequent days for these "mysterious illnesses." Poor job performance is typically the result of coming to work with a hangover or coming down from drugs in the workplace. The existence of a preoccupation of when the alcoholic or drug addict will be able to get high again can also act as a constant distraction from the job at hand. For those alcoholics and drug addicts who are unable to go without their drug of choice while at the workplace, they often find themselves victims of accidents. This has led to the proliferation of drug free workplaces where employers can benefit from lower workman's comp rates in exchange for mandatory random drug testing of all employees. For someone who is in early sobriety, a drug free workplace can offer an additional level of accountability despite the initial resistance of the newly sober alcoholic or drug addict to apply for such a position.

HONESTY –

As drug and alcohol addiction begins to dominate the individual, his or her basic values will begin to deteriorate as the addiction devalues the person. Honesty is replaced by lying, cheating, stealing and manipulation in order to protect the addictive side of the person as it gradually takes over. Honesty with oneself eventually is put into question, as the individual must rationalize being dishonest to others while at the same time protecting the addiction through denial. Sobriety will create a need for the alcoholic or drug addict to look at his or her behavior more objectively. They can ask for forgiveness or demonstrate that their sobriety really does represent a lasting change with a reemergence of the values that have been previously overlooked. This alone should be enough for the sober alcoholic or drug addict to gain acceptance from those who have been hurt by the addictive behavior.

RESPONSIBILITY FOR LESS DISAPPOINTMENT –

Through their addiction, alcoholics and drug addicts become unreliable. When drinking and using become the priority everything else becomes secondary. Commitments and obligations fall by the wayside. This is partly due to memory deficits that result from the destruction of brain cells caused by the repeated use of addictive substances. Alcoholics and drug addicts will also lose interest in all activities that are not alcohol or drug related. The life of the alcoholic and drug addict represents one disappointment after another for friends, family, and most of all, children. While sobriety will not automatically guarantee an individual to become dependable, the opportunity now exists. In addition to sobriety, the former alcoholic and drug addict must become accountable to themselves and others and not make promises to others lightly unless they are willing to keep them.

PRIDE –

Pride is something we can feel when we no longer experience shame. Addictions are shame-based. The act of drinking or using alone does not include shame. It is the behavior that ensues. Also, the sigma that society attaches to alcoholics and drug addicts is shaming. Pride is a feeling that can parallel sobriety. As we experience more and more sobriety, we can experience increasing amounts of pride. To be amongst a small minority that succeeds at sobriety is quite an accomplishment. It can also foster hope in all those who are still struggling with their addiction.

ABILITY TO DEVELOP COURAGE, DRUG AND ALCOHOL FREE –

When we anesthetize our emotions with drugs and alcohol we are also numbing emotions that can play an important role in self preservation. Healthy fear is one of them. To have drug or alcohol-induced courage we are also eliminating a certain degree of fear. When this is combined with poor judgment is the result true courage or just plain foolishness? Drug and alcohol-free courage assume taking a calculated risk after carefully weighing the odds and then proceeding after we determine that those odds will lead to a favorable outcome. It is only with sobriety that we can attain the ability of having good judgment and, even then, there is no guarantee.

LESS POTENTIAL FOR DOMESTIC VIOLENCE –

We have already discussed the role that drugs and alcohol play in increasing impulsivity as well as decreasing inhibitions. It is for that reason that alcoholics and drug addicts have great difficulty controlling their anger. When anger gets out of control it has a tendency to escalate. What may have begun as a simple argument can lead to verbal abuse, throwing objects, and eventually physical abuse. The loss of inhibitions allows this escalation to occur. Not all alcoholics and drug addicts engage in physical violence but there is no question that as a group, physical violence is more prevalent amongst this population than in the population as a whole. Therapy, and anger management in particular, can be the solution for some. Frequent incarceration represents the solution for others. Sobriety in all cases will give the violent alcoholic or drug addict the ability to regain control of emotions, inhibitions, and to a lesser extent, impulses.

LESS POTENTIAL FOR CHILD ABUSE –

We all know how children can be exasperating in testing our patience. Our ability to handle our children is directly related to our ability to maintain self-control. Parents often exclaim how their children almost "made them" lose it. Some parents actually do lose it. When a parent loses control they find themselves in a position where their parental rights can be severed. In sobriety loss of control can be minimized. Our parenting skills are not enhanced by the excessive impulsivity that can result from alcohol and drug addiction. Another benefit that sobriety can provide in reducing the propensity for child abuse in our society is indirect. Since there is a very high correlation between children that have been sexually abused by their parents and those who later abuse their own children, the benefits of any reduction in sexual abuse can be cross generational.

RESPECTABILITY –

Alcoholics and drug addicts are also human beings and as such, have as much a need for respect as anyone else. Unfortunately, on account of their behavior as well as the stigma that society places on addicted individuals in general, they become the beneficiaries of very little respect. Poor self-esteem, which is widespread amongst alcoholics and drug addicts, makes self respect an elusive character trait. Without self-respect, respect for others can be very difficult to come by. The high incidence of incarceration of alcoholics and drug addicts also represents a significant component of shame that the substance abuser must endure. For those with drug or alcohol-related felony charges, the lack of respect continues long after the probationary period has ended. Most employment applications will specifically inquire about arrests, and felonies in particular. This makes employment for the sober drug or alcohol addict more difficult to obtain, thereby increasing the odds of another relapse. While respectability must be earned and sobriety will usually provide a conduit for respect, for the sober alcoholic or drug addict who also happens to have a record, any respect will be limited to immediate family and friends.

DESIRE NOT TO ENGAGE IN
SOCIAL ISOLATION –

Many alcoholics and drug addicts drink and use actively in the privacy of their own home (for those who still have a home). This gradual withdrawal from society is the result of social stigma coupled with ostracism from friends and family who do not approve of their addictive behavior. Alcoholics and drug addicts will also be very selective with whom they keep company. Their main criterion for friendship is based on whether their friends drink or use drugs like they do because their addiction feels less threatened by individuals who overindulge to the same extent as they do. The practicing alcoholic and drug addict will also not run the risk of being criticized by other alcoholics or drug addicts. The fact that their newfound friends may turn out to manipulate them or betray their friendship for drugs, alcohol, or money will not usually come into consideration. Misery loves company.

TO AVOID THE PARANOIA
ASSOCIATED WITH USING –

A number of drugs can induce paranoia amongst other side effects. The most common are marijuana and cocaine. Some of this paranoia may be due to the fact that drug addicts are participating in an illegal activity and that they become hypervigilant. Paranoid thoughts can result from purchasing drugs from drug dealers who do not have a reputation for being upstanding; from the fear of being arrested and sentenced to jail; and from individuals who are predisposed towards paranoia and who suffer from thought disorders associated with a psychiatric diagnosis. Many illegal drugs only serve to exacerbate a pre-existing condition in which paranoia is predominant.

DRUG AND ALCOHOL COUNSELING –

As drug and alcohol counselors, we are in constant contact with drug addicts and alcoholics at different stages of their addiction and at different stages of sobriety. As drug and alcohol counselors in recovery, this provides us with a constant reminder of the many hurdles and difficulties we have had to overcome in order to achieve our status as clean and sober professionals. The negative consequences of addiction that we can observe in our clients represents a mirror image of our own. This plays an important role in our own sobriety lest we lose sight of what we once were and what brought us to where we are.

HARDSHIP –

It is important here to distinguish between two types of hardship: The hardship that we have endured on account of our addiction and the hardship of others. Our own hardship will, of course, have a greater impact on us and will contribute to what they call in AA "hitting bottom." If we consider all the various forms of hardship that resulted from our addiction, this may serve as a significant deterrent in sobriety in order to silence the addictive voice that may be pulling us towards a relapse. When we take into account the hardship of others, the most logical approach would be to have empathy and compassion for those who are suffering from the same affliction. Maybe even use their example as an incentive to stay sober. To the practicing alcoholic and drug addict, their sense of logic is also under the influence. For them the hardship of others only serves as proof that they are not addicted, since others may be worse off than they are. Time will tell.

ACTIVITY –

Clean and sober activities play an important role in sobriety. For many alcoholics and drug addicts any activity that did not involve drinking or using was not considered worthy of their time. In sobriety, any new activity that is not linked to their addiction will act as a substitute for drinking and using as well as a positive outlet to spend their time. In early to middle sobriety, clean and sober activities have a more utilitarian function: To distract the alcoholic or drug addict from frequent and intense cravings without the need to succumb to the addicted voices that are so prevalent in the early stages of sobriety. Activities also fill a social role in that we are now faced with an opportunity to meet new people. Our judgment will then come into play as to whether these new acquaintances will be positive or detrimental to our new life as clean and sober individuals.

DESIRE TO MAINTAIN ENERGY –

All drugs classified as depressants are going to reduce our energy and motivation. On the other hand, all drugs classified as stimulants are going to provide us with increased energy. Recovering from alcohol and drugs will always involve a certain amount of time in which both energy and motivation are severely restricted by the effects of withdrawal. In sobriety our energy level should be more or less constant. Fluctuations can be accounted for by increases in activity. Also, since drugs and alcohol can be directly responsible for sleep disturbances, there is a positive correlation between poor sleep and low energy. If we do not exert ourselves, physically and mentally, fatigue will not be induced and not be necessitated. Most sleep disturbances will, however, resolve themselves once sobriety becomes more permanently established.

THE CHALLENGE OF ADVERSE SITUATIONS –

Alcoholics and drug addicts live chaotic lives. This is, at least, partially due to their addiction having a direct impact on their lifestyles. Financial problems can lead to evictions or frequent moves to more affordable housing. Cars can be repossessed leading to the need to find alternate methods of transportation. Legal problems can lead to court appearances and the sudden need to take time off from work. Incarceration will, of course, lead to extended time off from work. For the alcoholic or drug addict their lives revolve from one crisis to another. In sobriety, crises are somewhat limited to events that pertain to daily life and are no longer related to addiction. The alcoholic and drug addict already has a lifetime of experience with difficult situations. Crises are second nature to the sober substance abuser who is able to proceed methodically and rationally without becoming over emotional.

THE NEED TO ELIMINATE DEPRESSION –

It is a well-known fact that alcohol is a depressant. Why then, when we stop taking stimulants, can we become depressed? Relatively speaking, the sudden absence of a stimulant, particularly an addictive stimulant, will make us feel depressed. In time this depression will either resolve itself or need to be treated with medication. If depression is left untreated, the need to self medicate with the substance that caused the depression will lead to relapse and a return to our drug of choice.

THE NEED TO FEEL BETTER –

It is ironic that alcoholics and drug addicts begin their drinking and using careers with the need to feel better, and it is their drug of choice that meets that need. Given enough time, not only does the addiction no longer make the alcoholic or drug addict feel good, but it can also play a nefarious role in the life and well being of the addict. Sobriety alone will not necessarily reverse that role, but it will provide a strong foundation for happiness that goes well beyond the realm of the addiction. To the alcoholic or drug addict, the benefits of sobriety can reach far beyond the initial desire to quit drinking and using. Once clean and sober, the recovering alcoholic or drug addict will very often determine if there are any other addictions that may be damaging to their health and need to be eliminated from what is now considered a healthy lifestyle. Smoking is probably the most common, as well as any cross addictions to drugs or alcohol. For some, food may be an addiction. For others, it may be caffeine. Gambling and sex may also be addictive behaviors that must be either treated or abandoned. While some drug and alcoholic treatment centers promote the simultaneous treatment of multiple addictions, personal experience has led me to believe that addictions must first be ranked in order of their potential for harm. Those addictions that are most life threatening should be eliminated first. This approach allows us to devote all our energy and concentration on being successful without being constantly distracted from our main goal. Giving up an addiction is stressful. Giving up two or three addictions at a time becomes unmanageable.

TO PREVENT DRUGS AND ALCOHOL FROM INTERFERING IN ONE'S LIFE –

As mentioned earlier, the alcoholic and drug addict suffers many losses as a direct result of their addiction. Some of these losses include relationships, children, personal values, spiritual and religious, material losses such as housing, vehicles, or personal savings and finally, employment including opportunities for promotion and the possibility of termination. While sobriety alone will not protect us from some of the vagaries of life, it will, however, play an important role in living life on life's terms without having to juggle an addiction, as well.

LACK OF MONEY –

Drug and alcohol addictions are expensive. They can also force us to make choices that are not always in our best interests or in the best interests of our families. When our personal resources become exhausted we must look elsewhere to finance our addiction. False promises, lies and manipulation now represent the fuel for our addiction, while limited resources and a distorted sense of priorities feed our addiction first and only give what remains to our families. Once we have exhausted all our resources and our ability to borrow money is tapped out, our ability to finance our addiction becomes compromised. Without resorting to stealing, the opportunity now exists to face our addiction directly and realize that what was once our best friend has betrayed us, and that we can now take measures to prevent such betrayal from occurring again. Sobriety now becomes an option along with the possibility and hope of regaining all or most of our previous losses.

GETTING BACK TO BASICS –

The need to get back to basics implies a return to values. Sobriety is a process in which the recovering alcoholic or drug addict must gradually learn to live again. It would be wrong to assume that the first day the alcoholic or drug addict stops drinking or using that he or she automatically achieves the status of "clean and sober." Sobriety is much more complex. On the one hand, it involves strategies to handle cravings effectively. It also involves the need to establish a sober lifestyle in which the need to drink and use will be eliminated. Getting back to basics represents the need for many alcoholics and drug addicts to start gathering all the building blocks that will be necessary for the foundation of their recovery. This would include being honest with themselves and others; being able to ask for help when they need it; becoming reliable and dependable with friends, family and employers; having courage to face fears drug and alcohol free; practicing good mental health for any coexisting psychiatric conditions; learning how to feel again and the role emotions play in our lives; learning how to handle negative emotions without resorting to drugs and alcohol; practicing good stress management and learning to be happy once again.

LOOKING FOR A NON-ADDICTIVE SUBSTITUTE –

When alcoholics and drug addicts give up their drug of choice a tremendous void is left in their lives. The tendency to substitute their drug of choice with another addictive substance is prevalent. This new addiction will usually not meet the need of the alcoholic or drug addict, and will precipitate a return to their original drug of choice. It is recommended that when we give up something that has a negative impact in our lives, we replace it with something positive. For example, someone with shortness of breath as a result of smoking or an anxiety disorder can take up running once enough time has elapsed to recover from the physical symptoms of smoking. It is also recommended that alcoholics replace their addiction with water. The tendency to use a substance that dehydrates will now be replaced by a substance that hydrates. There is also a psychological factor that ties into our subconscious. The frequent hand-eye movement of raising a glass to our lips and putting it back on the table can be repeated with water without creating a psychological disturbance that could, otherwise, cause a relapse. Alcoholics and drug addicts can also use positive reinforcement in order to help them along in their sobriety. We can calculate the monetary cost of our addiction on a weekly basis; set that money aside (preferably in some sort of savings account) with the goal of purchasing an item that, in turn, will have a positive impact on our life. This could be a car, a TV, a stereo system, an engagement ring, or anything that we would have liked to have but that our addiction prevented us from having.

HOPE –

Hope is one of the main ingredients in sobriety. When we have hope, we are motivated. Everything seems possible. Hope keeps us going. It allows us to put one foot in front of the other. It is why someone who relapses frequently will keep on trying until they get sober. Hope is what some of our friends and family have no matter how desperate our situation can be. Hope is the belief that despite the many losses from our addiction we will be able to recover some of them if we work hard enough. When we lose hope, our life loses meaning. We become depressed, maybe even suicidal. It becomes difficult to find any motivation. Life becomes a struggle. A dark cloud hovers over everything we do. Desperation sets in. Sobriety may now seem like a viable alternative.

DOING THE DISHES –

Something as mundane as dishwashing can have an indirect impact on sobriety. It can represent one of those distracting activities that we can practice when we are feeling cravings and the need to distract the mind from its addictive impulses, pleading and rationalizations. It can also be a useful tool for stress management. When the dishes are piled up almost high enough to touch the ceiling, doing the dishes will relieve all the mental stress of having to tackle a task that appears insurmountable.

MANAGING ANXIETY –

For many people, anxiety represents a trigger for drug and alcohol use. The two substances that most people with an anxiety disorder gravitate towards are alcohol and marijuana. Since we cannot feel anxious and relaxed at the same time, and since alcohol and marijuana tend to induce relaxation, dependence on these two substances can occur quite naturally for the anxious person who is seeking relief from their discomfort. What is less commonly known is that addiction to marijuana and alcohol can cause anxiety, particularly during withdrawal of these two substances. There is even a diagnostic classification entitled "substance induced anxiety" whereby the anxiety goes into remission when the substance that initiated the anxiety is no longer used. There are many more effective ways of treating anxiety other than developing a dependence on an addiction. Deep breathing exercises can be effective when they are used early enough to counteract the first signs of anxiety. Since anxiety can exhibit many symptoms, but shortness of breath is commonly shared by all, it stands to reason that deep breathing can be beneficial to everyone. Another technique that requires a little more experience is visualization. Here we develop a relaxing script, rehearse the script and review the script in detail every time anxious thoughts enter our awareness. Other relaxing methods of dealing with anxiety include prayer, meditation, massage, listening to relaxing music, reading, and physical exercise. Exercise induces relaxation through the release of endorphins and can have a residual effect long after the exercise is over. Staying present and not speculating about the future would be a good method to avoid negative thinking about the future and assigning negative outcomes to events that may never even occur. Thought stopping is also a practical method to eliminate negative thinking and maybe even replace negative thoughts with positive ones. There are also many different medications to treat anxiety. Many of these are highly addictive and would not represent the first treatment of choice for someone who already has a history of substance abuse. The entire category of Benzodiazepines would best be avoided. In addition, alcohol will potentiate the effects of these medications considerably while, inversely, the medication will substantially increase the effects of the alcohol. Some of these medications, when mixed with alcohol, can even cause death. Some of the more widely recognized benzodiazepines include Xanax, Librium, Valium, and Klonopin.

REALITY –

Most alcoholics and drug addicts take their initial plunge into their drug of choice in order to reap the benefits of oblivion. Drugs and alcohol have the "perceived" advantage of making us forget what troubles us. On an emotional level, drugs and alcohol numb the negative emotions associated with loneliness, boredom, anger, and depression. What the alcoholic or drug addict does not take into consideration is that positive emotions are equally numbed. In sobriety we are taught how to deal with negative emotions without self medicating. This allows us to feel the full range of emotions including those emotions that we value most. We can sometimes put reality on hold in order to buy some time while we decide how to cope with a particular situation, but we cannot run forever. Sooner or later reality will catch up with us. Some problems, if dealt with immediately, can be resolved with relative ease. Others increase in complexity over time and can only be resolved with great difficulty. Procrastination, a common strategy used to postpone reality, is only a minor form of avoidance. If we are able to know what the future would be like in advance, procrastination may be justified but how do we know if putting things off to a later date will be preferable to getting things done now? Reality, with both its positive and negative elements, should not be avoided but welcomed. In many ways reality should be accepted and embraced for what it is. When we decide to run away from it, it will still be there to greet us when we get back.

ENJOYING NOT BEING HIGH –

This allows us to enjoy the opportunity of not coming down from drugs or alcohol. A sober person will never suffer from withdrawal symptoms. A sober person will never worry about getting arrested for DUI. A sober person will never worry about waking up in the middle of the night on the bathroom floor in a pool of vomit. A sober person will have both the energy and motivation to participate in activities that he or she enjoys. Not being high also gives the recovering alcoholic or drug addict the opportunity to take part in activities that their drug of choice would not have permitted them to do. Addiction, in many ways, represents a forced choice. All other alternatives are not even options for the substance abuser.

LIGHTEN UP –

Our addiction makes us take life too seriously. Maybe because once we begin to experience the ravages of our addiction there is very little in life that is not serious. In sobriety we must learn to lighten up. Having a good sense of humor can lessen the stress of everyday life. Reader's Digest even has a regular column entitled "Laughter." The ability to lighten up can transform a somber atmosphere into a positive one.

Laughter can also be contagious. This explains why people like to be around funny people. For the alcoholic who used to drink in order to become more loquacious, sobriety gives them an opportunity to learn how to socialize without the liquid courage that he or she has come to depend on.

BECOME MORE PATIENT –

Patience is what we need in order not to fall victim to frustration, anger, or rage. Patience also represents a strong antidote to impulsivity. Lightening up, as previously mentioned, can be an effective means of developing patience. The Alcoholics Anonymous slogan of *One Day at a Time* is based on patience. Sobriety does not come to us in a neat little package. It must be nurtured and cultivated. We do not want to get ahead of ourselves. Acceptance can also play an important role towards the development of patience. The serenity prayer from AA addresses this well. Patience is one of those things that we can never have enough. We learn patience from our children. A good method used to extend our patience when we feel that we are about to run out is deep breathing. To be able to self induce relaxation when we need it most is an extremely valuable technique.

MAINTAINING A HEALTHY SKEPTICISM –

Skepticism is a character trait that is most often developed in childhood. Dysfunctional families and dysfunctional parenting are a good breeding ground for skeptical values. If a child should question a parent about a particular issue and the response is "because I say so," this tends to promote skepticism as well as the inquisitive and curious nature of the child. These values are maintained through adulthood and serve an important role in discriminating between information that is either factual or fictional.

TO ACCEPT CHALLENGES AS THEY PRESENT THEMSELVES –

Practicing alcoholics and drug addicts have great difficulty dealing with challenges. Some alcoholics and drug addicts have difficulty with daily life, let alone challenges. Addictions offer such a great opportunity to escape. Procrastination is also a much more attractive solution to problems than taking the time and effort to deal with life's challenges effectively. Sobriety on its own will not solve any of these problems. Sobriety will, however, offer us an opportunity to think clearly, make sound decisions and have good judgment. Our probability of success is much greater when we are sober as opposed to self-medicating problems that will not go away on their own. It is only our perception that leads us to believe that these problems are no longer in awareness. In reality, they are hovering around us and will soon be demanding a solution if one is not provided promptly.

CHILDREN –

To some alcoholics and drug addicts the mere presence of children has a sobering effect. This may be on account of their innocence or maybe a desire not to drink or use in their presence. When children are present we may have moments when we are transported back to our childhood. We may have a desire not to drink or use in their presence in order to, at least for the moment, pretend to be a good role model. It may also be possible that we recognize the negative impact of our addiction on ourselves and, even if we are unable to attain sobriety, it may be something that we wish for our children. For parents to wish a better life for their children than they had is a natural phenomenon.

MEDITATION –

We all have the ability to meditate, however, few of us will tap into this inner strength to attain a relaxed state of being. This is perhaps cultural. In our society meditation is not as popular as in eastern cultures. There are many benefits to meditation: Stress management, anger management, anxiety reduction, increased ability to focus and concentrate along with an increased ability to tolerate frustration and a greater ability to be patient. Meditation can also be used in relapse prevention as a form of distraction when those addicted inner voices are beckoning us to drink or use. For some, meditation has a spiritual significance giving us the ability to get in touch with our higher power. For others, the ability to achieve peaceful relaxation in a life where stress and chaos are routine can be comforting and soothing.

MEMORY IMPROVEMENT –

Alcohol and drug use destroy brain cells. Prolonged alcohol and drug use will cause major brain damage, leading to memory loss and cognitive dysfunction. When brain cells are destroyed, they will not regenerate. The damage is permanent. Sobriety will eliminate any further destruction and give the brain a chance to reorganize. Since at any given time we only use a small part of our brain, which our addiction has rendered, for the most part, inoperable, sobriety gives our brain the ability to tap into its unused portion and form new neuro-connections. As these neuro-connections are used increasingly, they begin to form new neuro-pathways. These neuro-pathways are essential for the formation of memory. While recovery may not be complete, it may be sufficient to enable us to go on through life with minimal dysfunction. For those of us with chronic long-term drug and alcohol abuse, the damage may be so severe that sobriety will not be sufficient to offset the cumulative damage that our brain has endured from our addiction. Some recommended techniques to improve memory and enhance our ability to retrieve information are crossword puzzles, reading, and the use of mnemonics.

A SUDDEN REALIZATION THAT DRUGS AND ALCOHOL ARE NOT THE PANACEA THAT WE ORIGINALLY BELIEVED THEM TO BE –

When drugs and alcohol are used in the initial stages of our addiction they appear to be very appealing. The effective numbing of negative emotions and the high or buzz that we feel become repetitively sought after. At this stage we are able to function reasonably well until we become dependent on our drug of choice. We are no longer drinking or using for any purpose other than to satisfy the addiction. It is at this stage that many of us realize that what started out as an effective means of self-medicating has become a serious problem that has robbed us of our freedom and independence. Only sobriety will be able to liberate us from this dependence.

MUSIC –

Music can be an effective tool for sobriety. Both playing and listening to music can manipulate our mood, so we must be careful on what we select if music is going to have a positive effect on us. Certain types of music can be very relaxing while other types can be stimulating. As recovering alcoholics and drug addicts, not all music is appropriate for us. Drinking and drugging lyrics may appear to be subtle on a conscious level but may subconsciously trigger a relapse. A good example of this is Jimmy Buffet, whose numerous ballads extol the virtues of alcohol. Some music that we hear in sobriety can also bring us back to the time when we first heard that music in an altered state of mind. This, too, may trigger a relapse on a subconscious level. Awareness represents our greatest defense against subconscious relapses that are triggered by music and the euphoric recall that music might induce.

FAITH IN MYSELF –

As our sobriety continues to gradually strengthen, we become more and more confident in our ability to maintain our sobriety. While this self confidence is justified, we must guard against the risk of overconfidence and the potential for relapse. Evidence of overconfidence can be seen in behavior that previously would have made us uncomfortable. We are now willing to take risks that we were unwilling to take before. We become impatient and impulsive instead of letting our sobriety guide us and pace our recovery. Overconfidence is probably the second leading cause of relapse after stress. In early sobriety the alcoholic or drug addict still identifies him or herself as a drinker or drug user, despite the clean and sober status that he or she has just achieved. As confidence increases proportionate to clean and sober time, there is a gradual conversion in identity from drinker and drug user to clean and sober individual. Once this new identity becomes internalized, the risk for relapse becomes more remote.

MYSELF –

In sobriety there is a need to state the obvious. We cannot take anything for granted because many of us in early sobriety are very much influenced by external forces. This can be a spouse, an employer, a relative, our children, a friend or a probation officer. In early sobriety our sobriety is weak and our denial is strong. We must derive some of our motivation from somewhere else. We are fortunate to have some people who still care. As sobriety progresses we experience a conversion from external to internally based motivation. This is where the recovering alcoholic or drug addict becomes self aware, self-motivated and self-confident, in short, self-reliant.

THREAT OF VIOLATION OF PROBATION –

I have yet to meet a recovering alcoholic or drug addict who likes jail. The threat of returning to jail can be a powerful tool for someone to remain compliant with the legal system. Some alcoholics and drug addicts are able to get some good clean and sober time while in jail. This can be used as a springboard to launch their sobriety. Other alcoholics and drug addicts fantasize every day in jail about drinking and using and the very first day of their probation they fulfill their fantasy. For some alcoholics and drug addicts it is the fear of getting raped in jail that represents a major disincentive to drink or use while under probation. In any case, the threat of violation of probation is a good motivator to remain clean and sober initially, and for some, a stepping stone for long-term sobriety.

SOS (SECULAR ORGANIZATION FOR SOBRIETY) –

The only requirement for SOS is a desire to stop drinking or using. This is not a twelve-step program. SOS was founded on the principle that sobriety is a separate issue from religion. Religious members are welcome in SOS but should not expect to find any discussion of religion in the groups. Members of all faiths are welcome but expected to practice their faith outside the group. Sobriety is to remain the priority and the group believes in self-empowerment. Having a higher power is not required to be a member of SOS. Individual members are also encouraged to share any issues they might be having regarding mental health. These issues are very much related to sobriety, since self-medicating a mental illness with drugs or alcohol is practiced by 60% or more of all individuals diagnosed with mental illness. SOS groups end by all members holding hands and applauding themselves and one another for their efforts towards becoming or remaining clean and sober individuals.

MAINTAIN SOBRIETY –

Alcoholics and drug addicts are accustomed to chaos. In the absence of chaos some alcoholics and drug addicts may have difficulty functioning. Their lives gravitate from one crisis to another. Sobriety gives them an opportunity to become stable, but this will require some effort on the part of the alcoholic or drug addict. Adaptation to a new lifestyle will require discipline. Priorities must be realigned in order of importance. Routine must be established. Self-imposed structure represents another method to remove any barriers that a chaotic lifestyle would have imposed on the alcoholic or drug addict. Good work habits must replace absenteeism and tardiness. With stability, the life of the alcoholic or drug addict will become more predictable. A reputation of being unreliable and undependable will be replaced with one in which reliability and dependability become synonymous with the alcoholic and drug addicts' new work ethic. From time to time a crisis will occur, but the alcoholic or drug addict will be able to draw on his or her past experience and then return to the stable lifestyle to which he or she has become accustomed.

NOT TAKING ANYTHING FOR GRANTED –

To the alcoholic or drug addict, sobriety is the key to life. Without sobriety we will not have anything. It becomes just a matter of time before all our previous losses will begin to add up. All the gains and all the efforts we made will be for naught. The bottom that we previously hit in our addiction will be challenged by new lows. The progressive nature of our addiction will make it a race against time before we seriously begin to contemplate homelessness. What can be worse than homelessness? Death, the last and final destination of our addiction.

WHITE KNUCKLING –

White knuckling is an expression used to describe abstinence without any further attempt at becoming sober. We have all met some alcoholics and drug addicts who are miserable without their drug of choice. I have even heard some people say, "Why don't they go back to drinking or using if they don't have any quality of life by remaining abstinent?" Sobriety gives us the ability to become functional. Abstinence gives us the opportunity not to drink or use only – for those of us who have chosen abstinence over sobriety, it is only a matter of time before our addiction increases its allure and draws us back to an even more miserable life than we had before.

RELAXATION –

To the alcoholic and drug addict, drinking or using represents their only form of relaxation. In sobriety it will become necessary to replace the role of drugs and alcohol with something equally if not more effective. Relaxation can also be very effective in reducing stress and anxiety, both triggers to relapse. Some commonly used methods for relaxation include visualization, progressive relaxation techniques, deep breathing exercises, massage, music, reading, meditation, yoga, tai-chi, taking a warm bath by candlelight or basking in the sun. It is important to strike a balance between relaxing activities and those activities that are physically more challenging such as aerobic exercise, which can also be important for our health.

NOT GIVING UP –

Long-term sobriety can be very difficult to attain. Statistically the chances of success are significantly lower than the chances of failure. Once someone has been seduced by the allure of addiction, it remains a viable option at all times. The addictive voices are constantly beckoning, especially in early sobriety when the rate of relapse is highest. For the individual who has had multiple relapses coupled with multiple failed attempts at sobriety, the possibility to give up is often contemplated. This is where the individual's support system can be of the utmost importance. If a close friend or family member should give up, the recovering alcoholic or drug addict is one step closer to losing hope. If he or she should give up on sobriety and give in to addiction, the individual would be embarking on a downward spiral potentially leading to homelessness and death.

LIVING LIFE ON LIFE'S TERMS –

Alcoholics and drug addicts, through their drug of choice, escape from the reality that life presents. Not only does this fail to resolve their problems but now they must face a whole set of new problems emanating from their addictions. Sobriety teaches us to face these problems without resorting to mind-altering substances. When we are successful, we gain the self confidence necessary to resolve issues of even greater complexity. This process is also helpful at raising self-esteem, which is typically lacking in alcoholics and drug addicts.

NOT BEING ON PROBATION –

To the alcoholic or drug addict, probation is a common occurrence. Getting awoken at 3 a.m. to be taken to jail for violation of probation (VOP) is an occupational hazard of addiction. Having one's life restricted and having to account for all movements to a probation officer represents a major loss of freedom that extends beyond the initial jail time. These and other unpleasant circumstances can lead the alcoholic or drug addict to want to avoid jail at any cost. The rigors of probation can have a sobering effect on the alcoholic or drug addict who may be unwilling to repeat the experience of probation and any further incarceration.

OPTIMISM –

Optimism is a positive disposition, possibly related to temperament, that some of us have the good fortune to enjoy. Optimism has a very high correlation with hope. For those of us who are fortunate enough to be optimistic, no matter how desperate a situation may be, we are always able to foresee a positive outcome. For most of us, optimism is something that is reserved for us in our sobriety. When we are in the throes of our addiction and we are faced with one challenge after another, can optimism be realistic? Also, since most recovering alcoholics and drug addicts have a tendency towards depression, can feelings of hopelessness and despair lead to optimism or would these be mutually exclusive instead? As the recovering alcoholic and drug addict goes through the early stages of sobriety, they begin to see some good things start to happen. This, in turn, gives them hope towards the future. Optimism becomes more feasible and is gradually reinforced as sobriety progresses onwards.

HAVING AN ESCAPE PLAN –

To the recovering alcoholic or drug addict whose judgment can be questionable at times, having an escape plan is essential. For an escape plan to be necessary we must first have been aware that we were about to engage in a risky situation. Since, at the time we formulated the escape plan we were aware of the risk involved, why should we venture into a risky situation in which an escape plan is needed in the first place? It is possible that, subconsciously, our addictive mind is acting behind the scenes to expose us to situations in which the addiction may take over. An example of this may be a decision to attend a party where alcohol and drugs would be available. The escape plan may be the decision to leave early if the addictive voices begin to get too strong. The risk is that the voices become so enticing that instead of leaving early we decide to stay and relapse instead. Good judgment would have dictated avoiding the party altogether.

ASKING QUESTIONS –

When an alcoholic or drug addict first decides to get clean and sober, he or she embarks on a totally new experience. For many, their only previous experience with sobriety was in childhood and early adolescence. Ironically, since any change is stressful, sobriety will initially cause stress until it becomes more established and actually begins to relieve alcohol and drug-related stress. For the newly sober alcoholic or drug addict, he or she is going to have many questions about his or her addiction and sobriety. This is one reason AA or NA recommend a sponsor. Many alcoholics or drug addicts may be embarrassed to ask questions in their respective meetings for fear of being ridiculed. The role of the sponsor is to give an opportunity to the sponsored individual to speak openly and fearlessly.

GROWTH –

Drug and alcohol addiction will act to arrest emotional growth. When emotions are effectively numbed, emotional growth stagnates. Spiritual growth also would be unable to grow in an unfavorable environment. With sobriety, both emotional and spiritual growth are no longer encumbered. Since emotional growth is arrested at the onset of the addiction, emotional growth will resume and continue to grow from the onset of sobriety. Complete emotional recovery is within the realm of the alcoholic or drug addict but not before intermediate to long-term sobriety is achieved.

ONE DAY AT A TIME –

To the recovering alcoholic and drug addict in the early stages of sobriety, just the thought of living the rest of their lives drug and alcohol free can be overwhelming. As a matter of fact, the loss of an addiction can be compared to the loss of a loved one. The grieving process is the same. For those alcoholics and drug addicts with underlying anxiety disorders, this can be quite disturbing. If they have come to rely on drugs and alcohol for short-term relief of symptoms of anxiety and they are now drug and alcohol free, what are they going to do now? This thought alone can trigger intense feelings of anxiety. The concept of one day at a time, which was originally established by Alcoholics Anonymous (AA), is recognized for its simplicity. We all have a tendency to complicate our lives more than we need to, while some of us tend to get ahead of ourselves. Living our lives one day at a time keeps us grounded in the present. Anxious thoughts about the future become superfluous. Living one day at a time makes sobriety more manageable and eliminates some of the self-imposed stress that we bring upon ourselves.

ELIMINATE NEGATIVE FACTORS IN LIFE –

If we cannot be happy in sobriety then addiction becomes a more attractive alternative. After all, what do we have to lose? Answer: Everything we didn't already lose before. Sobriety gives us an opportunity to put our life back in order. Little by little, we are able to eliminate all those factors that had a negative impact on our lives. Some of these factors include bad relationships, smoking, addictions to other substances, obesity, and mental illness. When we eliminate these negative factors, it is also important to replace them with positive factors. Once we have eliminated all negative factors, does that imply that happiness remains? Not necessarily, but it will be much easier to achieve happiness when we are not constantly carrying negative baggage.

ABILITY TO DERIVE PLEASURE FROM THE LITTLE THINGS IN LIFE –

No one can be happy all the time, but if we are able to derive pleasure from everyday occurrences, we can substantially increase the likelihood of happiness. Some examples include the sight of children playing, a smile, a pretty flower, spotting wildlife, noticing a funny situation, being optimistic by realizing that even though a negative event has occurred in our life, something much worse could have happened, and being grateful for what we have as opposed to wanting what may be unattainable. This does not mean that we cannot appreciate some of the major events in our lives such as the birth of a child, marriage, a birthday or a job promotion but these events occur seldom. True happiness depends on having a positive attitude and making a concerted effort to find happiness where others may find oblivion.

DELAYED GRATIFICATION –

Our society demands immediate gratification. While it is important to get our needs met, instant gratification raises an important question – what now? Is it not more satisfying to work hard to achieve a goal than to have everything handed to us? Is it not more satisfying to prepare a good meal than to microwave a frozen dinner? If sobriety was easy would we be as proud as we are for overcoming all the odds and resisting the many pitfalls and temptations of addiction? Delayed gratification also teaches us patience. We are able to set our sights on a goal and work diligently towards that goal. If we must delay our gratification, that goal becomes much more meaningful than if it is accomplished without the benefit of considerable effort and hard work.

ABILITY TO FOCUS AND REMAIN FOCUSED –

For alcoholics and drug addicts who are used to avoiding reality even when there is no need to do so, sobriety provides them with the ability to think clearly, make sound decisions and practice good judgment. This will, at first, take some effort on the part of the recovering alcoholic or drug addict. The brain damage that has occurred over years of abuse is not going to be reversed in the first days of sobriety. Making sound decisions and practicing good judgment will take some time and effort before becoming effective and reliable. As sobriety gains some strength in our lives our ability to focus and remain focused should increase proportionately.

PETS –

In order to take care of the physical needs of a pet, we must be able to take care of ourselves, at least minimally. Addiction to any substance will render this task impossible. The addiction must constantly be nourished at the expense of all other things. Aside from general maintenance, pets have emotional needs too. They need a certain amount of attention, love and caring that only a clean or sober individual can provide. Pets are also able to recognize the many changes in behavior that result from addiction. They are able to sense that there is something unusual with the person that cares for them and this can result in fear and avoidance. Sobriety can restore faith that pets have in their master. In many ways pets react in a very similar fashion as humans where addiction contaminates relationships.

GOOD CHOICES –

To drink or use or not to drink or use, that is the eternal question facing the alcoholic or drug addict. When we are drinking or using, we have a choice. The choice not to drink or use is implied and always rejected. In early to middle sobriety, we have the same choice but this time we choose to remain sober. From time to time, however, that addicted voice, which has been silenced a long time, will break through and lead us to relapse. In long term sobriety we still have the same choice, but this time it is the option to drink or use that is implied and automatically rejected. In early sobriety, awareness that we have a choice will lead to better decisions. When our addiction is on automatic pilot, we must take control of our options and begin to make good choices. Once sobriety is established, our ability to make better choices is enhanced by a clear mind, better thinking and the absence of mind-altering substances that reduce the effectiveness of our thought process and destroy brain cells that are essential for recovery.

NOT GROWING UP –

As adults, the stresses of daily life and the implied need to act maturely make us abandon some childlike characteristics that would otherwise serve us well in sobriety. The ability to be playful is one. As adults we have a tendency to take life too seriously. This does not mean that when serious matters arise we should act irresponsibly but, at other times, there are plenty of opportunities to be playful, take things in jest and approach life with a sense of humor. As clean and sober adults we often find children an inspiration to our sobriety. By not growing up, we are able to tap into our inner child and produce some of those same characteristics that can be found in our children.

Another trait that is often found in children but often neglected or abandoned in adulthood is creativity. Children have a good sense of imagination and this represents one of the main components of creativity. Some adults are able to nurture their creative side and develop lucrative careers as a result of their creative genius. For most of us, though, creativity remains a lost art abandoned in childhood, never to be seen again. This ability to be creative can be revived, once again, by looking to our inner child for guidance and inspiration.

STAYING AWAY FROM "UMBRELLA DRINKS" –

Umbrella drinks are those sweet tropical drinks where the alcohol is disguised by the flavor of fruit or some other ingredient. Bloody Marys also fall into the umbrella category even though they are "umbrella-less." To the sober alcoholic there is an inherent risk in ordering any of the nonalcoholic versions of these drinks. Bartenders, waiters and waitresses can and do make mistakes. Is it worth risking our sobriety on one of these drinks? Also, many recovering alcoholics enjoy the cool refreshing taste of nonalcoholic beer. Perhaps some are able to handle this without being tempted to try the authentic version. For others, psychological factors may reintroduce the addictive voice and trigger a relapse on what began as an innocent indulgence.

NOT TAKING LIFE TOO SERIOUSLY –

For those of us under persistent stress and unremitting anxiety, this can represent quite a challenge. Attempting to find humor in situations where, on the surface, there is none can represent quite a task. With practice and some effort this challenge can be met. The tremendous load that we were carrying now appears to be lighter. This, in turn, will make it easier to deal with those difficult issues that once appeared to be severely burdened. Friends and family will benefit, too, as we previously appeared overwhelmed. We are now, at least occasionally, relaxed and emotionally unencumbered.

AVOIDING THE PITFALLS OF HOMELESSNESS –

To the alcoholic and drug addict who is still in denial, homelessness is not something they are willing to relate to or even consider. It is true that many alcoholics and drug addicts will "hit bottom" a long time before they even come close to becoming homeless. It is also true that the streets and parks are full of alcoholics and drug addicts, who were unable to arrest the downward spiral of their addiction and are now using the streets for whatever shelter they might find. A small number of alcoholics and drug addicts are homeless by choice. They have found it easier to live a life without any responsibility and minimal expense. A little panhandling can go a long way for someone who is homeless. While some nonprofit agencies have been set up to help the homeless, many prefer their independent lifestyle to being bound by rules and regulations that have been artificially imposed by society. While many alcoholics and drug addicts have trouble relating to homelessness, they should still be aware that homelessness remains a distinct possibility if their addiction is allowed to continue untreated.

RECOVERING FROM ALCOHOL AND DRUG-INDUCED PHYSICAL PROBLEMS –

To the alcoholic or drug addict, it is only a mater of time before physical problems begin to surface. An unhealthy diet coupled with malabsorption of nutrients and insufficient exercise will lead to an impaired immune system. Being frequently exposed to the general public represents a depository for influenza, colds, infections and an assortment of bacteria. More serious problems include gastritis, ulcers, hepatitis, cirrhosis of the liver, pancreatitis, cardiac arrhythmias, cardiac arrest, seizures, and peripheral neuropathy. Other physical problems that are indirectly related to drug and alcohol use include accidents, HIV, AIDS, and other sexually transmitted diseases that are the consequence of an impaired immune system and promiscuous behavior that results from poor impulse control related to drug and alcohol use.

THE SERENITY PRAYER –

How often do we get stubborn and frustrated when we try to put a round peg in a square hole? How often do we get entrenched in an argument only to find that the other party is just as stubborn as we are and that the conversation will not get anywhere. The Serenity Prayer made popular by Alcoholics Anonymous and Narcotics Anonymous is a useful tool for relapse prevention, anger management, anxiety reduction and just plain common sense. The key to the Serenity Prayer is awareness. The sooner we become aware that something cannot be changed, the sooner we are able to accept it. We often think of the Serenity Prayer when it is too late or sometimes not at all, even though it always remains at our disposal.

KEEP IT SIMPLE –

Modern day life can be very complex. Dealing with the complexities of modern day life increases our stress load. Since stress is the leading factor to relapse, why do we frequently make our life more complicated than it needs to be? There are certain events or circumstances that we cannot control, while others are well within our sphere of influence. It is in our best interest to keep things simple whenever we can. Technology is advancing at a very fast pace. Why are we compelled to chase something that is going to be obsolete shortly after we obtain it? If it is for our job we might not have a choice but if it is for our personal life we do have a choice. Why do we feel the need to acquire material goods just because a neighbor or friend already has? If we have a legitimate need for them or if they serve some utilitarian function, why not – but if the only real purpose is to follow others like sheep we can simplify our life by refraining to purchase these goods. Everything we buy must be cleaned or maintained. This takes time, and time has become a valuable commodity that is in shorter and shorter supply. Since stress is a function of not having enough time to do the things we need to do in order to be competent and reliable, we need not overburden ourselves with goods that serve no real purpose in our life but to detract from those things that do.

IDENTIFYING AND AVOIDING HIGH RISK SITUATIONS –

To the alcoholic or drug addict, awareness can be crucial to sobriety. For the inexperienced or newly sober alcoholic or drug addict, awareness is not enough. The addictive voice will try to influence the uninitiated alcoholic or drug addict into participating in high-risk situations. This addictive voice must be silenced and rational thought processes must be used to override the addictive voice and maintain sobriety. Some examples of high risk situations include attending a party where we know in advance that alcohol and drugs will be available, renting an apartment in a crack neighborhood supposedly because the rent is cheaper, or getting together with an old friend with whom we used to drink or use. As we gain clean and sober time, the risk in all these situations will decrease with experience. Why should we take any risk if what we worked so hard for might be put into jeopardy?

KNOWING YOUR TRIGGERS –

In order to know our triggers one must first know oneself. To know oneself we must first be honest with ourselves. This requires a complete introspection of ourselves with particular attention on denial. Did we overlook anything that is going to be important to our sobriety later? If so, will that make us more vulnerable to relapse? Triggers are those conscious and subconscious places, people or things that represent a direct relationship to our addictive past and awaken the sleeping giant that is in all clean and sober alcoholics and drug addicts – our addictive voice. Subconscious triggers can be very subtle. Music where lyrics proclaim the benefits of getting drunk or high can have a seductive effect on our addictive voice and lure us back into our addiction. Money has been frequently cited as a trigger for cocaine addicts as well as any white powdery substance that will be mentally substituted for their drug of choice. Are we able to avoid these and other triggers in order to remain clean and sober? Not unless we can isolate ourselves completely by dropping out of society and avoiding all radio and television. This, of course, is not practical nor would it be desirable. The key to handling triggers is being aware of them and being prepared to deal with them when we encounter them in our lives. It is when we are caught off guard that our impulsivity is invoked and relapse is only a short step away.

SPONSORS –

Sponsors are only recommended in Alcoholics Anonymous (AA) and Narcotics Anonymous (NA). The use of a sponsor is substituted by a phone list in Secular Organization for Sobriety meetings (SOS). The principle of getting a sponsor is a good one. We can all stand to benefit from someone who has more experience than we do. It is usually a good idea to get a sponsor who has more sobriety than we do. The concept of same sex sponsors is also a good one. The principle behind this premise is to avoid any romantic entanglements too early in sobriety, while emotions are only beginning to be released from years of being numbed out by drugs, alcohol or both. The question about same sex sponsors does not, however, address the possibility about homosexuality and how that could lead to the very romantic entanglements that we were trying to avoid in the first place. Also, as knowledgeable as a person may be about their own personal addiction and sobriety, the individual might not have a very good understanding of what their sponsored individual has gone through in their addiction and is going through with their own sobriety. Another area of potential concern is the strong tendency for alcoholics and drug addicts to be codependent. If this codependency is carried over into their relationship with their sponsor, it does not bode well for any hope of independence in the future. All this notwithstanding, there are some very caring and concerned sponsors, who offer good advice and help a lot of fellow alcoholics and drug addicts.

TELEPHONE –

The telephone can serve many purposes. It can be used as a means to fight loneliness. The old advertising slogan "Reach out and touch someone" comes to mind. All drug and alcohol recovery groups encourage their members to use the phone to speak to one another regarding issues concerning their sobriety. Alcoholics Anonymous (AA) and Narcotic Anonymous (NA) require their members to get a sponsor and then speak to them regularly over the phone or in person. There are, however, some instances where the phone can be misused. Calling a drug dealer, for what amounts to setting up a relapse, is typical of such misuse. It is recommended to those clients who have used drug dealers in the past, to get a new phone number and destroy any phone numbers that could have a deleterious effect on their sobriety.

EDUCATION –

The more we know about our addiction, the more prepared we will be in our sobriety. Education includes reading the various pamphlets found at meetings, buying a self-help book about our addiction or some related topic, or auditing a class at a university or junior college on addictions. Education can also mean attending continuing education classes as a requirement for professional licensure. Some of these classes are also available to the public, sometimes even free of charge.

KEEPING WHAT WORKS –

At times it may appear that we are bombarded with information. We must be very selective in what we choose to keep. Knowing ourselves, which includes all our different strengths and limitations, represents a very good place to start. It is usually a good strategy to go with our strengths first, until we have time to work on some of our weaknesses. We may even choose to ignore some of our limitations altogether. The process of selection depends on a number of factors: Likes, dislikes, personal preferences, ability, prior knowledge, convenience, practicality, motivation, energy level, mood, degree of impairment, experience, sense of urgency and a willingness to try something new. As we continue down the road of sobriety, we begin to accumulate a number of strategies that work. We continue to add new ones as they become available to us. Sometimes we discover that some strategies that have worked in the past do not work all the time. We must let our experience dictate in which particular situations we can apply those strategies that are not always effective. To keep what works we need a positive attitude and an open mind in order to sift through all available options, before deciding which one will work and retain it for future use.

GETTING RID OF WHAT DOESN'T WORK –

We are once again stating the obvious at the risk of it being overlooked. In this case, we must be honest with ourselves. We must keep our old nemesis, the addicted voice, in the back of our minds. There is nothing that the addicted voice would like more than to see us commit to strategies that do not work. This would increase the opportunity for the addicted voice to make inroads into our sobriety and eventually take over and control us. We must be able to predetermine those strategies that will not work by self assessing how these strategies can relate to our sobriety and our personal traits and characteristics. If there is a poor fit, the best strategy of all might be to pass on this new coping skill and leave it to others who might be better able to use it.

PARTICIPATION –

Group participation, while recommended, cannot be required. For some alcoholics and drug addicts, attendance alone represents a major breakthrough following years of denial. Participation depends on trust, and trust can take a long time to develop. It is often a good strategy to begin to participate in a group by discussing a topic of low intensity and of little personal risk. As experience becomes increasingly positive, participation can become more meaningful. In any case, the right to pass or the right to keep certain information personal should always be respected.

TREATMENT –

Not every alcoholic and drug addict requires treatment. There is a small minority who are able to quit drinking or using without the benefit of treatment. Others need multiple treatment episodes and interventions and are still unable to become clean and sober. Treatment can be a very effective means of educating the client about addiction as well as sobriety, and represents for some, the initial stages of sobriety. Different treatment settings vary from least restrictive (outpatient) to most restrictive (inpatient). Intensive outpatient treatment programs also exist for those who need to work, but need more intensive treatment than the one hour per week outpatient programs. For those who are contemplating attending yet another treatment program after multiple treatment episodes, they may be relying on the treatment program to keep them clean and sober instead of being personally responsible for their sobriety. Treatment works if we make it work. The information in all treatment programs is basically the same. For addicts who have attended an assortment of different programs, there comes a time when they must apply what they have learned. For them to attend another treatment program will only mean more of the same.

Another important component of treatment is self-help groups like AA, NA, and SOS. Some alcoholics and drug addicts are able to get clean and sober by attending these groups alone. Others need a combination of treatment and self help. It is important that the information provided by the different modalities of treatment is different from the self-help groups, which are free of charge. Who wants to pay for something that you can get for free?

LEARNING FROM EXPERIENCE –

Early to mid-sobriety is typically when most relapses occur. Alcoholic and drug addicts are relatively inexperienced in their sobriety. They are still unable to deal with cravings effectively and, because of the recency factor of their addiction, they are still drawn back to behavior that has yet to be fully extinguished. Theoretically, as the alcoholic and drug addict gains more and more experience in dealing with his or her addiction, the time between relapses should increase until eventually the alcoholic or drug addict is no longer prone to relapse and sobriety establishes itself as the new pattern of behavior.

REMEMBERING –

This can be very challenging for alcoholics and drug addicts who have experienced many years of cognitive impairment resulting from the permanent destruction of brain cells from years of drug and alcohol abuse. For those of us who are fortunate enough to still have enough neurochemicals in our brain to allow us to function, remembering is what allows us to learn from our experience. Since sobriety is a learning experience, remembering plays an important role. If it were not for remembering and the ability to learn from our mistakes, we would repeat the same mistakes over and over again. It is also important to remember where we came from. After many years of sobriety, it is easy to lose sight of some of the many negative consequences of our addiction; the pain and suffering that we have endured and caused others; the shame and self loathing and poor self esteem that had become an integral part of our being, and the self-destructive behavior that is characteristic of our addiction. While it is important not to dwell on this, it must remain indelibly etched in our awareness, for it is this awareness that can help prevent relapse in mid to late sobriety. How often do we hear about someone with ten, fifteen or twenty years of sobriety or clean time who falls victim to relapse? A majority of these relapses would probably not have occurred, if they had been able to recall the great devastation and destruction that their addiction had caused.

SERVICE TO OTHERS –

Alcoholics Anonymous has always been a big proponent of service to others. While we are helping others, we are also helping ourselves. For another alcoholic or drug addict to need our help, they must be at a less advanced stage in their sobriety than we are. This acts as a constant reminder of where we were. Giving back also represents an expression of gratitude for the help we had received, when we were in our moment of greatest need and our ability to help others with the experience we have gained since then. Sobriety is a gift. Once we have received that gift, it can be passed on to others.

SERVICE FROM OTHERS –

While it is true that some alcoholics and drug addicts are able to quit drinking and using without any external assistance, this represents a very small minority. Most of us need some help and are grateful to get it. Some of us, even with help, are unable to remain clean and sober. Accepting help from others can be very difficult. The typical male upbringing in our society does not view asking for help as a viable option. As men, we must first try to solve our own problems. This would be a good approach for everyone to follow, but for how long? Is asking for help considered to be admitting defeat? Does getting help diminish in any way our accomplishments towards becoming clean and sober? The problem with dealing with sobriety on our own and without help is that the longer we remain in our addiction, the harder it may be to become clean and sober. To be stoic and ego syntonic may be positive male character traits in some cases, but not when they interfere with the overall wellbeing of the individual. This may very well just be a case of plain stubbornness.

OPEN MINDEDNESS –

Alcoholics and drug addicts spend a lot of time pursuing their favorite hobby, drinking and using. When they become clean and sober there is a tremendous void in their lives. If they don't fill this void with clean and sober activities, there is a strong possibility for them to return to familiar behavior. Having an open mind will give them an opportunity to try new activities. If these activities do not appeal to them, open mindedness will again allow them to try something different until they are able to find something satisfying that meets their personal criterion. To be open minded can also be helpful in the task of making new friends. This does not necessarily mean that we should like everyone that we meet. It also does not mean rejecting someone based on one or two character defects. Open mindedness can be used in accepting people for who they are. True friendship will ultimately be determined by mutual interests, our ability to communicate and resolve conflict satisfactorily when it presents itself and respect for one another, including differences as they occur.

WILLINGNESS –

The key to any major change is willingness. For the alcoholic or drug addict to be successful in their newly sober lifestyles, they must have the will and the desire to quit more than the will and the desire to continue drinking and using. While willingness will not always guarantee success in sobriety, lack of willingness will guarantee failure. The concept of willingness parallels that of motivation in that both represent inner strengths upon which we draw on order to accomplish challenging tasks that would otherwise appear to be insurmountable. Perseverance is also related to willingness. While willingness provides the initial impetus for change, perseverance allows us to remain on task until the change has been completely effectuated.

DAILY PLANNING –

For alcoholics and drug addicts, how they plan their time is essential. Free or unplanned time can be their enemy. Idle time can equate to an invitation for relapse. We can build relaxation and leisure time into our daily planning. All free time must be structured, for when boredom sets in we become receptive to self medicating our emotions. Daily planning can also be useful in managing stress. Setting priorities, organizing ourselves and planning daily activities can take some of the edge off of stress. Stress is the leading cause of relapse for the alcoholic or drug addict. Anything we can do to de-stress will have a positive influence on our sobriety.

HOMEWORK –

The alcoholic or drug addict must always be prepared. We must be able to anticipate treacherous situations or suddenly find ourselves in relapse. For this to occur we must do our homework. If we are planning on going to a party or a social event it would behoove us to find out if drugs or alcohol are going to be available. If we should still decide to attend, we need to know if any other clean and sober individuals will be attending. We will also need an escape plan in case things do not go as anticipated. While this may not meet the typical criterion of party planning, these activities are entirely appropriate for relapse prevention.

INVENTORIES –

Drug and alcohol addiction carries substantial wreckage in the life of the alcoholic or drug addict, as well as the lives of all those around them. It is generally considered a good practice in sobriety to attempt to rectify as much of the damage as we can. Sobriety gives us the ability to do so. Even though the addiction was responsible for our actions, we are ultimately responsible for our behavior. There is nothing better than having a clean conscience, doing the right thing, making amends, asking for forgiveness, repaying an old debt and, most important of all, demonstrating over time that we have changed our ways once and for all. These represent options at our disposal for cleaning up some of the wreckage that our addiction has left behind. Taking inventory allows us to think back on the past and list all the problems that need to be addressed in sobriety. We must also bear in mind that the memory of the alcoholic or drug addict is not always reliable. For that reason, we must learn to depend on collateral sources in order to reconstitute accurate representations of historic events that are either partially or completely out of our awareness.

USING YOUR THINKING SKILLS –

To the alcoholic or drug addict, this may not be as obvious as it seems. Our ability to think has been clouded by many years of drug and alcohol use. Our memory has been impaired by the daily destruction of brain cells on a long-term basis. It takes years to reestablish new neurochemical pathways in order to promote and accelerate recovery. We must attempt to use our mental capacities as often as possible. While thinking skills may at first seem somewhat primitive, frequent use will increase our ability to think and make better decisions as well.

H.A.L.T. – HUNGRY-ANGRY-LONELY-TIRED –

Yet another expression coined by Alcoholics Anonymous. The acronym H.A.L.T. stands for hungry, angry, lonely and tired. All of these feelings can make us vulnerable to relapse. Our ability to self regulate or manage these feelings will increase our likelihood to remain sober. Hunger can be very similar to cravings for alcohol or drugs. It would be very easy to misinterpret hunger for a craving and relapse based on this erroneous assumption. Anger is an emotion that is frequently self-medicated by drugs or alcohol. For those of us who have this tendency, anger management might present a viable alternative to relapse. Loneliness represents another "negative" emotion that frequently requires the company of alcohol or drugs. While this does nothing to solve the problem, it numbs the emotion so that it becomes less noticeable. Some practical solutions to loneliness include calling a friend, visiting a neighbor, friend or family member, or even listening to TV or the radio for company. Feeling tired or fatigued will reduce our resistance to relapse and make us vulnerable to stress, and eventually our drug of choice. Strategies to reduce fatigue include maintaining regular waking hours and sleeping schedules, taking a power nap when possible, practicing good sleep hygiene, including the elimination of caffeine and alcohol prior to bedtime and gradually decreasing our level of stimulating activities before bedtime, in order to promote an environment conducive to restful sleep.

LEARNING TO LISTEN –

In early stages we are all very inexperienced in matters related to our sobriety. Since we all have the ability to learn from each other, we must develop our listening skills in order to benefit from the prior experience of others. This does not mean that we must play the role of silent observers. Any questions we may have should be welcome and may even remind the more experienced alcoholic or drug addict of questions he or she may have had when they, too, were facing sobriety for the first time. In addition, many alcoholics and drug addicts have a tendency to monopolize conversations. This is usually done out of fear that if the conversation is somehow controlled by the other party, emotions may be involved that the alcoholic or drug addict may find painful. In the past these emotions were numbed by drugs or alcohol but now, in sobriety, the alcoholic or drug addict might be vulnerable. This explains the tendency of the alcoholic or drug addict to monopolize conversations to avoid the possibility of experiencing painful emotions.

REPLACING OLD ATTITUDES OR
VALUES WITH NEW ONES –

Sobriety represents a completely new way of life for the alcoholic or drug addict. It becomes essential for the alcoholic or drug addict to abandon all those attitudes and values that were conducive to alcohol and drug abuse, while at the same time practicing those attitudes and values that promote clean and sober living. Some examples include incorporating stress management in our lives as an adjunct to relapse prevention, and utilizing preventive coping skills towards anxiety in order to reduce triggers for drug and alcohol abuse.

AFFIRMATIONS –

Alcoholics and drug addicts will develop poor self esteem as their addiction progresses from the early to later stages. As values are gradually substituted by their drug of choice, self esteem declines proportionately. If the addiction is allowed to progress unarrested, in the final stages what was once a human being with substantial worth has now become nothing but a shell capable of obtaining, consuming, processing and excreting the remains of their drug of choice. Affirmations can play a positive role in sobriety but maybe not in the final stages when it may be too late. Affirmations are used in order to address the poor self esteem in addiction and reinforce the self worth of the alcoholic and drug addict in sobriety. Affirmations are positive statements that we repeat about ourselves, until they become fully integrated into our subconscious. At first we might not believe these statements, which may lead us to abandon the exercise and dismiss it as not having any benefit. If we persist, however, the results can be impressive. What we believe about ourselves and how we view ourselves can have an impact on everything we do. Positive self-esteem can also give us the courage and self-confidence that we need to overcome some of the challenges in life that would otherwise be considered too overwhelming.

THINKING THE "BUZZ" THROUGH –

Practicing alcoholics and drug addicts are often very impulsive. It is the nature of their addiction that reduces inhibitions and promotes impulsive behavior. In sobriety we have a choice. It is the awareness of this choice that allows us, prior to drinking or using, to think about some of the consequences that our impulsivity may have on us. This can be a very useful tool in relapse prevention. While no one can predict the future with any degree of accuracy, the consequences of drug and alcohol use are predictable. While it is the predictability of the effects of drug and alcohol that make drinking and using desirable to the alcoholic and drug addict, the consequences of this use are often ignored. It is these consequences that make "thinking the buzz through" such a powerful tool for relapse prevention.

CHURCH –

For the alcoholic or drug addict whose addiction has gradually replaced his or her values, church can be a good place for values to be re-established. Sobriety is a good foundation for these values. For those alcoholics and drug addicts who attended church prior to their addiction, church can have a positive influence. Church and prayer can also be an important tool in order to circumvent cravings or silence our addictive voice, when it attempts to lead our sobriety astray.

PROBLEM SOLVING –

While we are in our addiction, we have enough difficulty functioning let alone solving problems. The brain damage that is the result of our addiction coupled with the intoxicating effects of our drug of choice reduce problem solving to a guessing game, as opposed to an informed decision in which the pros and cons are objectively considered and judgment is applied to solve the problem. Sobriety does not represent a solution to all problems nor does it lead to perfect judgment, but our chances of success as clean and sober individuals outweigh by far those that are exhibited by our addiction.

CONSTRUCTIVE SELFISHNESS –

In order to attain the status as a clean and sober individual, a certain amount of selfishness is needed. Since it is the self that has been ravaged by drugs and alcohol, it is the self that will need to be restored as it was, prior to the addiction. For this to occur a great deal of personal growth will be necessary. Is it wrong to help ourselves when the person that needs the most help of all is us? Is it wrong to want to improve our lives and be independent of substances that control our behavior and our lives? Is it wrong not to be a burden on our families and society by becoming self sufficient and self-supporting? If constructive selfishness is necessary for our sobriety, then maybe it would be wrong not to enjoy the benefits that it provides us.

SCHEDULES –

Alcoholics and drug addicts need structure. They need to put order into lives that were full of chaos. For this they need discipline, something that has been elusive throughout their addiction. Schedules can help restore structure, order, and discipline. For the practicing alcoholic or drug addict, meals have lost their priority. With a schedule, meals become part of a daily routine. They become regular and are taken at regular intervals. As with most rules, there are exceptions but schedules should help "normalize" the life of the alcoholic and drug addict. Sleep is another area that needs scheduling. First it must be determined how much sleep the individual requires. Also, at what time must the individual wake up? Do they need to be at work at a certain hour or do they have children that must be taken to school? This will determine the time at which they must wake up. From that time we subtract the number of hours of required sleep and we get our optimum bedtime. Will this guarantee a good night's sleep? No, but it will provide an adequate amount of time for sleep to occur.

BEING ASSERTIVE –

Assertiveness can be linked directly to self-esteem. This does not necessarily mean that everyone who has good self-esteem is necessarily assertive. However, few people who have poor self-esteem are going to be assertive. Assertiveness is often a reflection of a healthy ego. In some ways it is the ego that is the driving force behind assertiveness. Practicing alcoholics and drug addicts will typically have poor self esteem. This is the result of their addiction gradually eroding all their values. Assertiveness will teach the alcoholic or drug addict to stand up for their rights and defend their ego from external attack. This alone should have a beneficial effect on their self esteem and self worth.

HEALTHY ANGER –

Since anger can be a trigger for substance abuse, it stands to reason that if anger can be managed appropriately, relapse can consequently be avoided. Healthy anger includes all those coping skills that minimize the adverse consequences of unhealthy anger. Unhealthy anger includes using drugs or alcohol, verbal abuse, screaming or yelling, throwing objects or becoming physically or sexually abusive. Healthy anger includes counting to ten or one hundred, asking for time out, leaving the anger-provoking situation, venting, deep breathing, or engaging in some other relaxing activity. When we engage in healthy anger there is no need to abuse drugs or alcohol. Our emotions are being well managed internally and do not require any additional intervention by drugs or alcohol.

FOLLOWING DIRECTIONS –

Alcoholics and drug addicts have a problem with authority. This stems from a deep-rooted dislike for control. In sobriety, they continue to dislike authority and control and have trouble following directions until they are able to distinguish the difference between following orders related to their employment and being controlled by a parent or

101

caregiver. If authority and control can be attributed to a meaningful purpose, it might be more palatable to the alcohol or drug addict who has learned to resent this behavior that has been over-generalized.

PRIORITIZING –

Most alcoholics and drug addicts take life as it comes, living from hand to mouth and fighting life's challenges without anticipating the consequences that their addiction may have on their lives. When they get overwhelmed, they resort to drinking and using and everything appears to be ok, at least in the moment. When stress begins to build, the pressure becomes too great to handle and the alcoholic and drug addict will do what they know best – drink and use. Prioritizing gives us a chance to observe items in a logical fashion without getting overwhelmed. We only really need to focus on the first item on our list. All other items can be considered later. This removes the pressure of having too much to do and not enough time to do it all. If at the end of the day there are items that remain undone, we do not have to be concerned. Instead, they will find their way on the next day's list. Any strategies that help reduce or minimize stress will be effective tools for relapse prevention and sobriety in general.

MEETING AFTER THE MEETING –

It has been mentioned that meetings can play a very important role in the social life of the recovering alcoholic and drug addict. This role can be supplemented by the opportunity to get together after the meeting for a cup of coffee, or just to exchange ideas about addictions or any other topic that they may be willing to share with each other. They are also able to make plans to meet on another day of the week to participate in sober, recreational activities of their choice. From this, friendships can be formed and a common bond can be established to fight addiction and promote sobriety.

EFFECTIVE COMMUNICATION –

We are all able to communicate. We are not always able to communicate effectively. Communication does not mean just getting our point across. Listening skills can be just as important. Speaking and listening must not be biased by any preconceived notions or perceptions. For this to occur we must verify that what has just been said or intended is aligned with what has been understood. We must also guard against mindreading and jumping to conclusions. We must use our best efforts to prevent misunderstandings. Reflective listening is a technique that can be used towards that goal. The concept is simple but, as with any new behavior, it will need some practice before it becomes effective. Each person is to repeat, in their own words, what the other person has just said. This gives the other person an opportunity to clear up anything that needs clarification, or correct anything that may be ambiguous, awkward, or imprecise. This technique is used by each person, back and forth, and if adhered to by both parties, will serve to render communication effective and precise while eliminating misunderstandings and sources of conflict.

I STATEMENTS –

We live in a society where blaming appears to be a national pastime. Taking responsibility for our actions, especially when they involve negative consequences, can invoke fear and anxiety and is most often avoided. I statements allow us to be responsible for our emotions without blaming others. An example of this is when we say, "You make me angry." This clearly blames others for our own emotion. If instead we say, "When you try to control me, I feel angry," we are simply saying that it is the behavior of others that triggers an emotional response. We maintain responsibility for our emotions without the need to blame and the defensive posturing that would ensue.

ASKING FOR WHAT YOU NEED –

This is directly related to assertiveness. In order to take care of ourselves, we must make ourselves a priority. This does not mean that we must act selfishly without any regard for others. If we do not take care of ourselves, then how would we be able to take care of others? Also, how are others supposed to know what our needs are, if we do not make them known? In terms of gender, most women have been socialized into being nurturing and will not hesitate to ask for what they need. Men, on the contrary, have been taught that asking for help is considered a weakness and would rather remain helpless than allow their machismo to be tainted.

A RECOVERY PLAN –

To recovering alcoholics and drug addicts, sobriety is not a haphazard occurrence. For sobriety to be successful, there must be a plan. For the plan to be effective, it must be devised by the recovering alcoholic and drug addict and either their sponsor, their therapist or at least someone with more sobriety than they have. The plan can include any or all of the following:

- Number of meetings per week to attend (AA, NA, or SOS). This is usually more frequent at the outset and can gradually taper off as sobriety gains strength. Alcoholics Anonymous recommends 90 meetings in 90 days, which may work for some but may be excessive for others.

- Whether inpatient or outpatient treatment will be necessary depends on the occurrence of any previous episodes of treatment and the degree of success related to these episodes.
- The presence of any coexisting psychiatric disorders and the psychiatric stability of the alcoholic and drug addict.
- The degree and various sources of support that may be available to the alcoholic and/or drug addict and any environmental factors that may be relevant. Is the alcoholic employed as a bartender, waiter, or waitress? Does the drug addict live in a drug-infested neighborhood or near a crack house? Is the drug addict employed as a doctor, nurse, or pharmacist? All these factors require special consideration in the establishment of a recovery plan.

THE TERM "RECOVERING" ALCOHOLIC OR DRUG ADDICT –

This is an ongoing debate and will elicit much controversy. Popular opinion states that the term recovering alcoholic or drug addict must be used throughout the remaining life of the alcoholic or drug addict. The purpose is to serve as a reminder that we are only one drink or drug away from triggering our addiction. This is a valid point. From a perspective of growth, the implication is that the "recovering" alcoholic or drug addict remains sick or diseased (to use another controversial term). For those of us who have worked diligently on our sobriety for many years, for those of us who have eliminated any cross-addictions including nicotine and food, for those of us who have become asymptomatic of co-existing psychiatric disorders and have been in remission for many years, and for those of us who have crossed the line from dysfunctional to functional, the label of sick or recovering does not apply any longer. Does this mean that we are perfect and have reached nirvana? Of course not, but maybe a new label of "recovered" is deserved. In order to determine whether the term recovering or recovered is appropriate, I believe that we must consider the individuals premorbid level of functioning. If we are functioning at an equal or superior level in our sobriety than our level of functioning prior to the onset of our addiction, then what is it that we are recovering from?

TIME –

Alcoholics and drug addicts are always looking for a quick fix. When it comes to sobriety, there is no quick fix. Long-term sobriety, as its name implies, takes a long time and a great deal of experience. Finding out what works and what does not and discovering who we are as a person and then learning to like that person can be very challenging and time consuming but at the same time rewarding. Dysfunctional behavior and the underlying addiction that promotes it cannot be reversed overnight. Before we can exhibit any new behavior, we must first extinguish the old behavior and gradually replace it with more functional behavior. As we all know, change takes time and is also stressful. Having to deal with stress-related change will cause setbacks and relapses. This will compromise the recovery process and the time it will take before true sobriety can be attained.

LEARNING HOW TO SAY NO –

There is a tendency among many of us to practice people pleasing. This is when we put the emotions of others ahead of our own. We all have a need to be liked, but what about our need to like ourselves? When we practice people pleasing our self-esteem is externally based. When we like or love ourselves, our self-esteem is derived internally. While it may be nice to obtain recognition from others, it also makes our self-esteem dependent on others and at risk for being unfulfilled. Learning to say no maintains our integrity, creates boundaries, and can even earn the respect of others who recognize the value in dealing with someone who is not always a "yes" person. Learning to say no is also an essential component of assertiveness, which is considered to be the most effective means of communication.

STOP BEING A VICTIM –

We are not responsible for our addiction. It may be a disease, it may be hereditary, or it may be environmental. It may even be due to a combination of factors. We are, however, responsible for our sobriety. When we get caught up in the victim mode, we become helpless. Inertia begins to settle in. Victims show very little initiative. Their attitude becomes fatalistic. Victims often show signs of depression and hopelessness. Are victims always predestined for failure? Not if they take responsibility for their lives and their sobriety. For this to occur they must view themselves as survivors. Survivors have courage and resiliency. Survivors have the attitude that no matter what happens, they will be ok. Survivors believe that they will have the strength to overcome even the most difficult situations. It is this positive attitude that, when applied to sobriety, can make the difference between success and failure.

TALK YOUR PROBLEMS OUT –

For extraverted alcoholics and drug addicts, this may not seem like a difficult task. For introverts, though, this may seem to be close to impossible. The need to talk about our problems is not to overburden other people with our difficulties. Most problems are emotionally charged. As we discuss our problems, some of the emotion is released. Other people may also offer useful advice that would otherwise be inaccessible. For all we know, the person whom we are sharing our problem with may have already dealt successfully with that problem, unbeknownst to us. We all have a number of resources at our disposal. To ignore them is to willfully restrict the number of solutions at our disposal, when the optimum alternative may very well be the one that was never considered.

BECOME YOUR OWN BEST FRIEND –

Sobriety is all about rediscovery and self-acceptance. In our addiction we have alienated the self. In sobriety the self is nurtured. We integrate our inner child into our being. Our goal is to merge all those fragments that were once part of our life into one complete whole. Learning to love ourselves and accept ourselves as imperfect beings is a good first step in becoming our own best friend. Acting in our own best interests, determining whether something will have a positive or negative impact on us and how we ultimately view ourselves as opposed to what others may think about us will have a profound influence on how we become our own best friend.

REWARD YOURSELF –

Alcoholics and drug addicts reward themselves by drinking and using. In sobriety they must establish other methods of recognition or rewards. Southwest Florida Alcoholics Anonymous has a chip system where different levels of sobriety are rewarded by different colored chips.

The chip, of course, is symbolic of achievement in sobriety and is not only valued by the recipient, but all those who may be new to sobriety as it symbolizes hope. Anniversary dates also represent milestones in sobriety and can be celebrated in many different sober ways. SOS traditionally rewards its members by ending all their meetings by applauding themselves and one another for their efforts towards achieving sobriety. Some recovering alcoholics and drug addicts also choose to determine the monthly cost associated with their drug of choice, and set that amount aside on a regular basis towards the goal of purchasing a particular item that has been wanted or needed for some time. This could be a car, a new stereo system, an engagement ring or anything else. This will later serve as an ongoing reminder that sobriety was instrumental in the purchase of that item.

GIVING BACK TO THE COMMUNITY –

Practicing alcoholics and drug addicts become selfish the longer they allow their addiction to progress. This is not by choice but because their choices become more and more limited by an addiction that requires more and more personal resources. Sobriety is a gift. A gift that once received must be shared with others. Volunteering represents one of the best ways to give back to the community. It also represents a positive approach in order to counteract some of the selfishness that is inherent in addiction. Volunteering will also benefit the recovering alcoholic or drug addict by increasing self esteem. Helping others is time well spent and rewarding not just to others but to ourselves as well.

DEALING CONSTRUCTIVELY WITH
PHYSICAL AND EMOTIONAL PAIN –

Alcoholics and drug addicts typically have a low tolerance for physical and emotional pain. Whether the pain is severe or merely an exaggeration, they rationalize an urgent need to self-medicate. There are options available other than their drug of choice. Assigning a level of pain on a scale of 1 to 10 will determine whether medication should be an option. Low levels of pain can be dealt with without resorting to medication. A level of 2 or 3 can be tolerated without too much suffering. Pain management techniques can be helpful for all levels of pain. Since pain can cause tension, any method of relaxation should be able to reduce tension and make pain more tolerable. If pain is concentrated in a particular area of the body our attention will be focused on that area. By shifting our attention to other areas of our body and remaining focused on those areas, we should be able to effectively reduce some of the intensity associated with the original source of pain.

Emotional pain can be more severe than physical pain. Some people will even inflict physical pain on themselves in order to distract themselves from emotional suffering. This method is not recommended. For individuals who suffer from such severe emotional pain, they need to release their pent-up emotions in a safe environment. They need to discuss the source of their pain with someone they can trust such as a friend, a close relative or even a therapist.

WEIGHT LOSS/WEIGHT GAIN –

The body interacts with our drug of choice by either increasing or decreasing our metabolic rate (the rate at which food is metabolized by the body) depending on the substance we are using. Drug addicts who abuse stimulants will typically lose weight. Cocaine addicts, and women in particular, fear any weight gain that may result from getting clean. Smoking cessation will lower the metabolic rate when nicotine, a simulant, is no longer introduced into the body. The fear of weight gain has given many smokers a genuine disincentive to quit, despite the many health hazards associated with smoking, including death. Another factor indirectly related to weight loss is the fact that most drug addicts, while active in their addiction, do not eat food on a regular basis and are not very aware of nutritional requirements whenever they actually get around to eating.

For practicing alcoholics, alcohol causes malabsorption of nutrients, which are eliminated from the body before any nutritional value can be extracted. Alcoholics are also notorious for irregular eating habits. Since alcohol is a depressant, a low metabolic rate would be expected accompanied by a proportionate weight gain. But for reasons we mentioned above, the opposite holds true. In sobriety, since alcohol has a very high caloric content, the expectation would be for weight loss to occur, all things being equal. Why then do sober alcoholics gain weight? In sobriety good eating habits are restored and the caloric loss related to alcohol consumption has been replaced by improved nutrition and the calories associated with more regular eating habits. Also, sober alcoholics frequently not only crave alcohol but will also crave sugar, which has not been identified as harmful. As a result they over indulge in sugar and its high caloric content. In effect, they have substituted their addiction for alcohol with sugar. Another area of concern for the sober alcoholic is emotional. Many alcoholics, who have self-medicated their emotions in the past with alcohol, have now substituted food as a means to continue self-medicating while maintaining their sobriety. The result is a new addiction to food, which if left untreated, will lead to obesity and the many health risks associated with this disorder. The alcoholic will have gone full circle from sobriety and a desire for health to obesity, which can lead to diabetes, heart disease, strokes, and death.

GEOGRAPHIC CHANGES –

Alcoholics and drug addicts often decide that a change of scenery will be enough to break them from their addiction. While it is true that the drug addict will be leaving behind all his or her connections to buy drugs, the addictive voice will be clamoring for new connections soon after the addict settles down in his or her new surroundings. Geographic change only represent a change of scenery; for sobriety to be attained a major change must occur in the lifestyle of the alcoholic or drug addict. The practicing alcoholic may be physically able to relocate to a dry county, but the addictive voice will soon be pleading for a geographic change of its own, albeit temporary, to satisfy its thirst for alcohol. Another frequently unanticipated problem related to geographic changes, is that once the person relocates, there is a good possibility that loneliness will set in. Not only are the negative influences such as drug dealers and drinking and using buddies left behind, but so are all the friends. Another factor that does not bode well for geographic changes is the fact that change is stressful. When the stress that is caused by new surroundings is coupled with stress related to moving, getting a new job, learning a new job, and maybe even the stress related to finding a new drug dealer, a relapse may not be too far behind.

THE LEGAL SYSTEM –

Few alcoholics and drug addicts avoid either direct or indirect involvement in the legal system. For most of them this comes at a time when they can afford it least. Attorney's fees, court costs, probation fees, the cost of DUI school in some cases and mandatory rehab in most cases all contribute to overburden an individual whose addiction has already caused him or her to be financially tapped out. The threat of jail can act as a very real disincentive to drink or use, particularly for those who have already experienced incarceration. For some alcoholics and drug addicts their sobriety can get off to a good start in jail, as they are counting the days for their release. Drug court is a relatively new concept in which the legal system recognizes that incarceration without treatment only leads to very high rates of recidivism. The impending threat of jail for violation of probation may be enough to give someone a clean and sober start towards what could be a lifetime of sobriety.

WORK OR POTENTIAL LOSS OF WORK –

Work very often will represent the last bastion of stability for the alcoholic or drug addict. Work does not only represent a meal ticket, but also a steady source of income to the alcoholic or drug addict to finance his or her addiction without resorting to begging, borrowing or stealing. Work is very often the last thing to go in the life of the alcoholic or drug addict. The potential for loss of work can act as a powerful incentive for the alcoholic or drug addict to remain compliant with the rules of the workplace. In addition, many employers require their employees to adhere to the policies of a drug free workplace which include mandatory drug testing of all employees on either a random basis or based on suspicion of drug or alcohol use. The drug free workplace can be used as a tool for the newly clean and sober drug addict or alcoholic, in order to provide an environment that is conducive to their continued rehabilitation.

NOT BEING AFRAID OF BEING DIFFERENT –

We live in a society in which conformity is the norm. Any deviation from the norm can be met by ridicule and ostracism. Some alcoholics and drug addicts drink and use as an attempt to fit into society and be accepted. We are often concerned about what other people think of us.

This may be the result of a desire to please or maybe even the need to be accepted. Since we are unable to influence the thoughts of others, this represents an exercise in futility. Some people are able to accept us as we are, even though we may appear to be different from them. Others may value our differences and find us interesting because of them. In early sobriety the recovering alcoholic or drug addict is often preoccupied by what other people will think because they are not drinking or using. Few people concern themselves with the behavior of others as long as such behavior does not have any effect on them. In fact, many people might not even notice what someone is drinking unless they were previously familiar with his or her drinking history. Of all the people to be aware of the major change from drinking and using to sobriety, we are the most aware. Our new status as clean and sober individuals can make us feel very self-conscious. In this case, the difference is within ourselves and unrelated to the perception of others.

WILLPOWER –

It has often been said that if the desire to quit drinking and using is greater than the desire to continue drinking or using, the quest to be clean and sober can be attained. How can someone regain control from something as powerful as an addiction without willpower? Willpower requires saying no to alcohol and drugs on a consistent basis. Willpower equates to self-empowerment. Self-empowerment cannot take place without reasserting ourselves from the addictive process and consistently gaining the upper hand. Willpower cannot exist without hope. Of the many different coping methods that are addressed in this book, willpower is, by far, the most important one. A major component of sobriety is dependent on willpower. What is not directly dependent on willpower either complements willpower or can help prevent relapse independently of willpower.

ABILITY TO TOLERATE DISCOMFORT –

Alcoholics and drug addicts are constantly looking for an excuse to drink or use. They have a subconscious need to rationalize their addiction. When it became known that a client in a 28-day day program was going to the dentist the next day, 16 other clients developed mysterious toothaches overnight and signed up to go to the dentist. Other alcoholics and drug addicts will go to great lengths in order to obtain their drug of choice. An alcoholic prescription drug abuser self-inflicted 3rd degree burns with an iron in order to justify a trip to the emergency room as a result of her addiction. Discomfort is an indication that something must be done in order to bring us back to comfort. Discomfort can be physical, mental, or emotional. Most people have no difficulty handling discomfort. Alcoholics and drug addicts would not either, were it not for their addiction. There is an almost constant need for the addiction to be satisfied and the alcoholic or drug addict is constantly scanning the environment to satisfy this need. Also, if we constantly self medicate when we experience the least amount of discomfort, our ability to tolerate discomfort without resorting to our drug of choice is substantially compromised.

WHAT KEEPS YOU SOBER?

WHAT KEEPS YOU SOBER?

ABOUT THE AUTHOR

Prior to his retirement in February 2013, Roland Levy was a mental health counselor for 21 years. His primary specialty was dual diagnosis, where addictions and mental health diagnoses co-exist. He practiced in community mental health for 8 years and was in private practice for 13 years.

He lives in Sarasota, Florida with his wife Barbara and has a daughter, Violette, from his first marriage. His interests include reading, gardening, designing jewelry and silk flower arrangements and endurance cycling. He has been sober since July 14, 1989.

ACKNOWLEDGMENTS

I would like to thank the various group members for their dedication to their sobriety and their contribution to this book. I am also grateful to Christina Veillette-Nelson whose typing skills contributed to the original manuscript. I am indebted to Skip Weaver who provided suggestions towards the publishing of this book as well as Francis Lostys and Ann Di Cesare of Reader's Digest, whose life long friendship and support as well as editing expertise contributed to the editing of the original manuscript. I am also grateful to my wife Barbara and my daughter Violette whose willingness to provide technical support has allowed me to pursue my own personal sober activities without having to deal with the frustration and inefficiencies that are prevalent in our computer driven society. Many thanks to Jim Christopher, who featured the original manuscript in his newsletter. I am also indebted to my son, Billy, who has not been physically with me since 1998, but has provided me with ongoing inspiration and motivation in all of my endeavors.